SIMPLYEAT

EVERYDAY STORIES OF FRIENDSHIP, FOOD AND FAITH

SIMPLYEAT

EVERYDAY STORIES OF FRIENDSHIP, FOOD AND FAITH

First published in Great Britain in 2018

Instant Apostle,
The Barn,
1 Watford House Lane,
Watford, Herts
WD17 1BJ

British Library Cataloguing-in-Publication Data

A catalogue record for this book is available from the British Library

This book and all other Instant Apostle books are available from Instant Apostle:

Website: www.instantapostle.com
E-mail: info@instantapostle.com

ISBN 978-1-909728-94-3
Printed in Great Britain

CONTENTS

CONTENTS (CONTINUED)

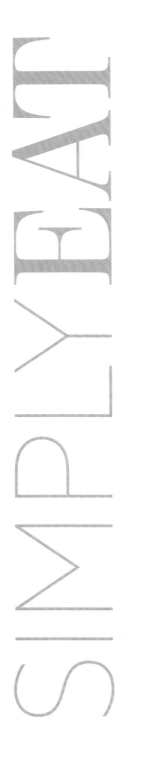

Why Simply Eat?

MANOJ RAITHATHA

I have always been passionate about food. I love to host people and take them out for meals. It is a way of showing love and respect that I inherited from my Asian culture. But it is only recently that I have come to understand how fundamental food and eating together are to friendship and faith.

I was raised a Hindu and first heard the message of God's love in Jesus Christ at primary school. My response was utter amazement. I had thought salvation was something one was meant to earn and couldn't get my head around the mind-blowing concept of grace. Brought up on Bollywood films, I thought it was the good guys who always won. But here in the Christian message I discovered a uniquely different story – God seeming to 'lose', limiting Himself to take on human flesh, the Creator dying for the created, the King for His servants. It was an astounding story and I was captivated.

But I was also young and other interests soon began to vie for my attention. Christianity was sidelined and money became my draw. I turned to a career in property trading to amass the wealth I thought I needed – only to lose most of it in the 2008 financial crash. At the same time as the crash, our son became critically ill. It wasn't the first time and we knew the drill: race him to hospital where he would be given the nebuliser and kept in for a few days and all would be fine. Except on this occasion the nebuliser failed to work. He was rushed into resuscitation where I vividly recall holding him as his airways shut down. He was intubated and later transferred to St Thomas' Hospital in London.

Over the course of the ensuing days, my wife and I wept for our son. On the fourth day, the doctor didn't have any positive news. It felt like it was one of those conversations preparing us for the worst. Nonetheless, I was hugely strengthened by the prayers of a Christian couple we had recently met and by their actions in galvanising others here in the UK and USA to also pray for him. This was the first time I had witnessed people praying for someone they didn't know and I couldn't get my head around such love. With all this resonating in my mind, to our utter disbelief my son suddenly bolted upright in bed no more than an hour after the challenging conversation we had had with the consultant. It was a miracle. My son was alive.

A few weeks later, I was walking to the front of a church and giving my life to the One who gave His life for me. I had allowed grace to slip through my fingers once before, but not this time. My mind was made up, God had heard those prayers and saved my son; but His own Son He had not saved. His own Son had gone to the cross so that all of us could have life – even I, who had ignored His grace for so long.

My new-found faith would take me into various areas of Christian work, one of them being the South Asian Forum at the UK Evangelical Alliance. We were focused on helping Christians share Christ with those of other faiths, but after a number of years it suddenly dawned on me that we were missing one of the most important components. Eating together! This had been crucial in my own journey to Christ, and it would be for so many others. One of the key things about the Christian friends who had prayed for my son was that they had regularly invited my family into their home for a meal. It was around food that genuine friendship and trust had been built, enabling us to go deeper in our conversations about faith. I distinctly recall one particular meal together after my son was healed where the conversation focused on the historical evidence for Jesus Christ. It was not long after that discussion that I found myself in church giving my life to Him!

With a keener interest in the links between food and faith, I was encouraged to hear other fascinating stories of Christians eating together to build genuine community and share the message of Jesus in natural and loving ways. It made perfect sense. Jesus always grabbed opportunities to eat with others and share His life with them – and so should we. *Simply Eat* brings these incredible stories together, celebrating the divine interplay between friendship, food and faith, and giving delicious and original recipes that make it happen.

This thought-provoking book has been made possible thanks to the generous support and partnership of London City Mission, Interserve, All Nations, the Church of England – Birmingham and the Great Commission and South Asian Forum teams at the Evangelical Alliance. Their collective input and wisdom has been essential to the shaping and production of *Simply Eat*. I would also like to thank all the contributors who have so willingly shared what God has done in their lives. Finally, a special mention to Nigel Freeman, David Salmon and Dayalan Mahesan for their oversight of the creation process, and the wider Instant Apostle team. Without their enthusiasm, hard work and creativity, there would be no book in your hands!

My hope and prayer is that the stories and recipes in this book will inspire you to rethink the power and place of food in celebrating faith, sharing Christ and building community.

But enough from me. Now to *Simply Eat*.

Faith-filled memories

Encountering Jesus Christ was a truly life-changing experience. My gradual realisation that this living and loving God was relational and not religious brought a deeper freedom than I had ever imagined possible. As a Hindu priest for twenty years, I had never known that God could be so close, personal and real.

I am thoroughly enjoying my walk with the Lord and the fellowship and love of new friends and 'family' that He has kindly built around me over the past six years. These are people I can trust and share with in an open and vulnerable way that I was never free to in my past life as a Hindu priest – indeed, I would never have dared to be so open with my fellow priests.

However, this doesn't mean that I do not value my old friendships. Quite the contrary, I muse over them quite frequently, particularly when I eat alone – something that very seldom happened before I became a follower of Jesus. In fact, my most memorable moments of being a priest are the fun times we had with food within the setting of fellowship.

Sharing food – and lots of food at that – and quality time spent around the table with friends and colleagues as a Hindu priest was both the norm and incredibly fun, yet also a strangely deep spiritual experience. There was something profound and precious about this seemingly trivial activity. Shared meals were the unplanned classes that brought fresh life within the complexity of our disciplined spiritual search. We all knew this as priests and yet we wouldn't have known how to articulate it if we were asked, because it was such an obvious and natural part of our spiritual journey together.

It wasn't a 'ritual' on our list of religious 'things to do' and yet it had its own unique and special place. There was a consistent emphasis from senior priests for us to eat together, which coupled well with Eastern culture's eating rhythms as a whole. In the years since I gave my life to Christ, amidst all the richness it has brought, this is the aspect of daily life that I miss the most. In fact, it is the only thing I miss about my previous life without Christ. Eating together regularly is a gaping hole that I see missing in general Western culture and the Western Church.

Fellowship and food were not something we talked about in my background. It wasn't something we had to put in the diary as an 'add on' activity to do on a weekday here and there. Instead, it was central to life, deeply entwined within the fabric of our everyday busyness. No matter how time-tight we were – and we were very tight with time – food and fellowship were never compromised. They were held firmly at the centre of everything, with the rest of life revolving around them. Even when we fasted from food, we all fasted as one, knitting our spiritual journeys together.

During my training years in the Hindu monastery in India, we were taught repeatedly, 'Your smart and intelligent sermons must never replace the importance of sitting with each other or members of the congregation amid an abundance of food.' Sharing food, the giving and receiving of hospitality, were understood to be profound ways of connecting with one another and

RAHIL PATEL

Fun with food – the missing ingredient

honouring one another. Letting a member of the Hindu congregation cook for you when you visited them and sampling all the dishes, sometimes dozens of them, was a way of incarnating any truth you might want to share with them in words. This practice is so reminiscent of how Jesus conducted His ministry. How much more, as those who know and follow Him, should we be practising this same kind of daily shared nourishment?

I did find it strange in my early years of being a Hindu priest how this food dynamic was emphasised again and again amid all of the other 'spiritual' tasks we had to perform. As I grew older and more observant, however, I saw the joy and satisfaction it brought, not just to the members of the congregation, but to me as well. It created a more mature sense of belonging and reassurance that all the other more 'spiritual' practices could not.

During our mealtimes in the Hindu monastery, we delighted in enjoying lavish feasts, with much celebration and laughter as we ate together. Now, this may sound very unspiritual to the religious mind, but I'll dare to say the opposite. This type of party or feast was very spiritual, and had a profound impact which reached way beyond the stomach. There's something very special about feasting, sitting amid abundance, and now, as a Christian, I can celebrate that any feast we have here is just a small foretaste of the great heavenly banquet that God will provide for us.

> A childhood attitude suddenly resurfaced that it wasn't 'our' food, but everyone's

Living and growing up in an Asian family in London, I remember when my relatives would make a phone call to our home. It amuses me today to think how simple and uncomplicated the exchange actually was. 'Are you home?' 'Yes,' I would reply. 'Fine. Tell your parents we are coming.' Without any formal invite or 'boundary-minding mindset', a whole group of people would be in my home with plenty of food constantly filling the table. Again, whether it was relatives or friends, once you had entered a home you would never ask, 'Can I grab an apple?' or 'Can I have some chevdo?' (Bombay mix). That would be an insult to the host. The culture was to simply reach out and help yourself to whatever you wanted and eat away.

Recently, I had the chance to visit Baroda city in India to meet my lovely grandmother. Here I was taken back to my childhood with amusement. My relatives and I were camped around the television with a fine variety of food, lazily snacking away. Suddenly our neighbours began strolling in through the open front doors – uninvited, of course! – sat down between us, casually helped themselves to our food and joined in the chit-chat. I was blown away and equally fascinated with the natural process of it all. A childhood attitude suddenly resurfaced that it wasn't 'our' food, but everyone's; anyone who walked through the front door had equal access. It was such a simple reminder, yet I realised this principle was something I'd sadly forgotten since becoming a Christian. Returning home, I've been inspired to consider what we can learn from this way of living to reinvigorate the heart of how we do community as Christians.

You might be thinking at this stage that Eastern culture and the large network of family and friends can be intrusive at times. I couldn't agree more. There is no concept of 'healthy' boundaries like we comfortably have in the West, and yet that very messy way of living out of each other's homes is strangely fun and attractive. I'll dare to say we are naturally drawn to it by design. It's that very messy place where a deeper level of reassurance, purpose and belonging resides, when we love one another in the way Jesus taught us.

This way of living is so prevalent in the Bible. I love stories of the early Church but I have noticed that we rarely mention how the disciples ate together and did life together. They never faltered or failed in the doing of family. I have visited Israel and seen the settlements around Galilee, which suggest a very intimate way of living. These days, food and fellowship seem to have been downgraded, sadly losing their place at the very centre of life from where revival pours forth, but back then, they were the fabric of Christian community. It can be hard to understand that we are one spiritual body when we so rarely share the vital experience of feeding our physical bodies together.

Food was significant to the way Jesus fellowshipped and lived; however, these precious moments of interacting with people are usually converted into metaphors for sermons today. The simple fact that He took time and ate with His disciples is often sidelined because it seems too simple. Yet the fact that eating together was so effortless and normal in Jesus' culture must not blind us to the power of the act. The disciples first belonged, being welcomed to share Christ's life and table, and thereafter believed. Their theology of the incarnated God followed the reassurance that Jesus was a practical part of their everyday life.

One of the first things Jesus did after the resurrection was to cook breakfast for His disciples. The crucifixion, resurrection and second coming are pivotal truths to those of us who follow Jesus. But isn't it fascinating that there's a communal meal associated with each of these crucial moments of salvation? If we learned to eat together more, I believe we would rediscover key elements of the kingdom – and have lots of fun too!

HELEN THORNE

Set free by a festive invitation

wasn't looking forward to Christmas. I never did. Family dynamics were always a strain during the festive season and that year things were particularly tough. I had a drink problem, and was out of control and self-harming, trying to 'sort things out' in my own strength and failing.

Just as I was hitting rock bottom, a lovely Christian couple noticed my pain and started to welcome me into their home. They fed me, encouraged me, told me they loved me even though I was in a mess, and said that even in the darkest of times, there was hope. I wanted to believe them. I wasn't sure I did.

On one visit, they issued an invitation: did I fancy Christmas cake, mince pies and midnight communion on Christmas Eve? It was a resounding 'yes' to the first two options – an awkward squirm for the third. I accepted nevertheless. Cake has always been a big motivator in my life!

I duly went round, enjoyed the sweet treats, and sheepishly followed them to church. I can't remember the passage I heard, I can't recall the talk, but I know beyond any shadow of doubt that I was captivated. Suddenly everything started to make sense. Their welcome, their generosity, their love, their overflowing confidence that the future could be different – all were rooted in this mysterious God come down. I didn't know who the baby in the manger was or why He grew up to be a man who died on a tree, but it seemed to me that He was key.

Life didn't change overnight. Many more conversations in their home had to happen first. But that simple invitation to cake and a communion service was a turning point in my life: from there the real journey from addiction to follower of the King began.

Come in and eat

Some time ago, my wife and I met a couple from a different culture and community and, wanting to get to know them better, thought about something we could find in common. Us being of Indian origin and them from Africa, we thought surely that common link should be food.

We invited them for a meal and cooked a big feast, including tandoori chicken, daal with courgettes and onion bhajis, to name just a few of the dishes. It was one of those meals that just really opened up conversations. We ended up spending three hours chatting and laughing with each other, and by the end of the meal felt like old friends – something that we have now become. I think it all stems from that first meal we had together.

I also relate food to my own salvation experience, as I'm constantly reminded of in Revelation 3:20. There Jesus says, 'If anyone hears my voice and opens the door, I will *come in and eat* with that person, and they with me' (my emphasis).

When I first read this verse I felt very humbled, as well as honoured, that the God of the universe wanted me to eat with Him! And that's the same feeling I had when I gave my life to Christ, awed that an all-powerful God longed to have a personal relationship with me. Just as my wife and I delighted in eating with our African friends, sharing our lives as we shared our food, so God longs to commune with us around the table – what an honour and privilege!

My Passover debt

I have such fond memories of eating the Passover meal at my grandparents' home as a child. My paternal grandfather, Aaron, led the Seder (the telling) of the Exodus story, but each one of us took part in reading a small portion of the tale. Passover united our family in a special way. Aunts, uncles and cousins I didn't often see sat round a large oak table; four generations reading the Old Testament together.

Inviting smells from the special food wafted from the kitchen. In pride of place on the table was the Seder plate containing six items that have a significant meaning. Firstly, a lamb shank bone, reminding us of the Passover lamb; a roasted egg, representing new life or sacrifice; salt water, representing the tears and sweat of enslavement; bitter herbs (maror), reminding us of the hard life the Israelites suffered under Pharaoh. Then there is charoset, a delicious mixture of nuts, apples and wine, representing mortar used to make bricks. Finally, parsley (karpas) representing spring and the hyssop branches used to put the blood on the doorposts of the Israelites' homes. In addition, there is unleavened bread (matzos), for all yeast must be removed from the house. And no Jewish meal would be complete without chicken soup, the recipe being handed down from mother to daughter for generations!

We also drank four symbolic cups of wine during the meal, representing the four expressions of deliverance promised by God to the Israelites in Exodus 6:6–7. The first, the cup of sanctification ('I will bring you out'), the second, the cup of proclamation ('I will free you'), the third, the cup of redemption ('I will redeem you'), and the fourth, the cup of praise ('I will take you').

These family Passover celebrations were wonderful times of laughter, reconnecting and exchanging stories. Instead of having to be quiet during the meal, we kids were encouraged to speak and ask questions. I was so grateful when my younger cousin was old enough to join in because, as the youngest, Passover tradition had meant that it fell to me to ask the special question, 'Why is this night different from all other nights?', and I was pleased someone else would now have to do it!

It gave Grandpa great pride to have the whole family around his table, and his eyes would twinkle as he handed around the four cups of wine, even to us children, and told the story in answer to our questions. By the end of the meal we were all convulsed in laughter as we sang the familiar Passover songs. But as soon as we got into the car for the journey home, my brother and I would be fast asleep until we arrived, well after midnight.

I owe a debt of gratitude to the enthusiasm of my grandfather. Those precious memories of his love of retelling the Israelites' journey to freedom to his family gave me the desire to read the Old Testament, drawing me close to God. And it was during a Passover meal that I realised Jesus was the true Passover Lamb, the promised Messiah of the Jews.

Now, I have the honour of sharing about Jesus from a Jewish perspective in Passover services with churches.

Chicken Soup Serves 4 to 6

Ingredients

1 medium boiling chicken or 4 joints of chicken

10 cups water

2 teaspoons salt

2 medium onions

4/5 carrots

2 sticks celery

½ teaspoon pepper

Matzo balls

Method

1. Trim fat from chicken, but don't remove skin.
2. Place chicken in a large saucepan. Add water and salt and bring to boil over high heat, removing scum occasionally from surface.
3. Add the onions, carrots and celery to soup, reduce heat and simmer, partly covered, for 1 hour.
4. Add pepper, and salt to taste. Simmer for a further 15 minutes, then remove from heat and cool.
5. Strain soup, reserving the vegetables and chicken. Refrigerate overnight.
6. Next day, discard layer of fat from surface of soup. Remove skin from chicken and dice meat for soup.
7. Reheat soup and add reserved vegetables, diced chicken and cooked Matzo balls.

'I am the bread of life.
Whoever comes to me will
never go hungry'

John 6:35

Learning the joy of hospitality

In the early days of my first marriage, my husband and I, together with our infant son, went to the Democratic Republic of Congo (then known as Zaire) to be missionaries in a remote location near the border with Central African Republic. We flew to Kampala, Uganda, and there had to wait at the mission headquarters until someone with enough room in their vehicle, who was heading to Zaire, would take us over the border.

After about a week of waiting, we were kindly driven through Uganda to the north-west and through the border to a large mission complex in north-east Zaire, called Rethy. Once again, we were to wait until someone could transport us further north. This never happened, as the day we arrived, the American nurse in charge of the hospital heard that her father was seriously ill. Since I was a nurse and midwife, I was taken on a tour of the hospital the next day, and from that time onwards, I was in charge!

That was scary enough in itself and gave many challenges, but as the days and weeks went by, I found this was only one of many duties expected of me as a female missionary. We were the only British family with our mission working in Zaire – all the rest of the expatriate staff were from the USA and Canada. British people tend to be more reserved and private – and I was horrified when I found that I was expected to do a lot of entertaining. I still needed my 'L' plates as a cook.

Not only were there several families, couples and single missionaries who lived at Rethy, there was also a school for the children of missionaries who lived all over the country and beyond. At the beginning and end of each school term, plus at half-term weekends, many parents would arrive, and they all needed to be housed and fed.

Sometimes, now, I look back and realise that the Lord allowed me to stay at Rethy because He wanted to teach me the joys and blessings of being hospitable. It was very hard work, and quite a challenge to stretch our meagre supplies to feed others constantly. We had no shops or supermarkets nearby – just a tiny paraffin fridge, which stored very little, and a wood stove on which to cook. I did have the part-time help of a very experienced young man, who was wonderful at getting the stove to the correct temperature I needed. I also found the soil was very fertile; my husband bought seeds from Kenya and we began to grow our own fruit and vegetables.

Gradually, the Lord helped me to change my attitude from resentment and anger to enjoyment when people arrived for meals. Sharing our lives and our table with so many others from different cultures and backgrounds enriched our lives. We made so many friends and some of them I am still in touch with forty-plus years later.

The children in Rethy Academy became our friends, too. They missed their parents, and although they had lots of fun and lovely dorm parents, they enjoyed being asked out to our home at weekends, and we loved to cook treats for them. A few of these children are also still in touch with me.

I have learned that the gift of hospitality is such a joy – and I still love to invite people round! It doesn't have to be gourmet food – a simple meal is just as acceptable. It's eating and sharing together that matters.

So, this is the recipe for the meat loaf I often served in Zaire.

Rethy Meat Loaf Serves 4 to 6

Ingredients

1lb minced beef

1½ teaspoons salt

Pinch pepper

1 egg, lightly beaten

2 slices dry bread, soaked in water, but not too moist

1 small, finely chopped onion

1 stalk celery, finely chopped

¼ cup chopped tomatoes or tomato sauce

Method

1. Mix all ingredients together and put into a greased loaf tin.

2. Bake at 200C/180C fan/gas mark 6 for 1 hour.

Generous gift of sacrifice remembered

I n my early twenties, I lived and worked in a rural village in Uganda for nine months. During that time, I experienced many different cross-cultural moments, and lots of them centred around sharing food. A meal that stands out to me was on an occasion when I went with my friend Godfrey to visit his uncle's family. As we made our way on our bikes, Godfrey kept expressing how excited he was for us to meet more of his family, and that we should be excited about the welcome we would experience.

On our arrival we were greeted by the whole family. It was a large crowd, and we were taken to meet Godfrey's uncle. Through Godfrey translating, we established that the family had been preparing a meal for us to share with them. As we'd cycled quite a long way, this was very welcome. However, what we didn't realise was the size of the meal that had been prepared. Different dishes kept being brought to the hut that we were in. There was goat, chicken, fish, matooke and much more – it was a feast! As the food kept being brought out, I shared my concerns with Godfrey about how much this meal would have cost the family, but Godfrey said it was their honour to be able to give us a meal, one that required great sacrifice on their behalf, a sacrifice they made because they wanted to make us feel welcomed.

Epitomised in this meal was the welcoming and hospitable culture I had experienced in Uganda. What has challenged me ever since is the sacrificial generosity that was shown to us, people who knew Godfrey but were complete strangers to his uncle and wider family. This selfless liberality challenges many of us in the West to re-evaluate what can be a limited understanding of hospitality and food. Theologian Robert Jenson writes in his second volume of *Systematic Theology*:

> *All meals are intrinsically religious occasions, indeed sacrifices … For all life belongs intimately to God, so that the killing involved in eating – which we do not at all avoid by eating vegetables – is an intrusion into his domain … Sharing a meal is therefore always a communal act of worship and establishes fellowship precisely before the Lord.*

We may not immediately relate a meal with the idea of sacrifice. Yet, whether it's the core principle of something losing life for us to be sustained in life, the financial sacrifice made by Godfrey's uncle to welcome us, or the sacrifice of time made by parents, grandparents and carers every day to prepare a meal for children, all meals involve an element of sacrifice. This self-giving that is inherent in any meal opens the way for healthy relationships to be built, for a willingness to put the needs of others before your own to be nurtured.

Given how we can understand eating together in terms of sacrifice, it is interesting that Jesus requested His disciples remember His sacrifice through the celebration of a meal, the Lord's Supper (Luke 22:19). The bread and wine symbolise the willing sacrifice He made of Himself to open a way for humanity to be reconciled with God, and the sacrificial elements in every meal can become a daily reminder of it, recalling God's generous gift in His Son. As Godfrey's uncle went to great cost to make my friend and me feel welcome, his sacrifice is a small reflection of how God's love led Him to pay the ultimate price to enable all of humanity to be welcomed around His table.

> This self-giving that is inherent in any meal opens the way for healthy relationships to be built, for a willingness to put the needs of others before your own to be nurtured

The Lord's Supper is a unique meal as we celebrate the new life we have because of Christ's sacrifice and the friendship we can now enjoy as we are reconciled with God and one another. It is the archetypal meal of worship because it is based on the ultimate sacrifice. It's also a meal that directs our attention forward. It points to the time when Jesus will return, when all things will be made new. A time that the Bible describes as a great wedding banquet.

Food and self-sacrifice are at the heart of healthy human existence and every meal is a religious occasion, which is why I think Jesus established this ritual of remembrance in the context of a shared supper. He knew this was something we would always do and He wanted to give us a way of continually remembering the love of God revealed in His sacrifice on the cross. Yet it further highlights the religious occasion of every meal because the sacrifices involved in all meals are a continual witness of this ultimate sacrifice, something we can remember every time we come together and simply eat.

'In the presence of the Lord your God,
you and your families shall eat
and shall rejoice'

Deuteronomy 12:7

Power to heal wounds

As I was growing up in the Caribbean, food was always important. I soon learned that getting together to do nothing but eat, drink and socialise – 'liming' – was vital to our community and way of life. This was never more evident than on excursions to the seaside. Only Caribs would rise at ridiculous times of the morning to board sweaty coaches and travel for hours to some of the most beautiful beaches in the world, only to sit in a hall or banquet room and consume copious amounts of food!

But it was not the actual food that made it worth missing the beaches, rather it was the preparation that went into making the meal and then sharing it together. This was the time for talking, reminiscing, laughing and, sometimes, shedding tears and reflecting.

Over time, I realised that coming together around food could often do more to heal wounds than words or actions ever could. Many who came on these trips were going through challenging times, but whatever the situation, people who came looked different on the way home. I could see it on their faces. Their loads had been lightened because they had been able to give and open something of themselves through the preparing and eating of a meal. 'Liming' is not just about eating – it is also about sharing who and how we are.

Surrogate mum

I n my early thirties, I became ill with what was later diagnosed as Ménière's disease. But the agoraphobia – the fear of leaving my home or immediate vicinity – was more crippling than the illness. Because I was so unwell, I lived with my mother. Despite having a relationship, studying at London Bible College (as it was called then), and planning to go into full-time ministry, suddenly, my life was broken. The relationship was over, I was unable to work, go to church – or go anywhere. But God drew very close and opened a door for me to become an author and later an editor – a testimony too long to go into here.

My health improved and in time I was able to go to church again. But sadly, my mother became ill. She was told she had epilepsy, but actually the seizures were being caused by small strokes. Very quickly she was in a home with vascular dementia and Parkinson's disease.

What a shock! It had happened so fast. My bright, lively, witty, independent mother was now in a wheelchair, her mind virtually destroyed.

Around that time, I joined a house group, which was being held not far from where I live, in the home of a lady called Maria. Maria is a remarkable woman. She was born in southern Italy but has been in the UK since childhood. A talented interior designer, still busy though past retirement age now, she has worked for many influential people. She and her gifted husband, Alan, are also excellent cooks. They are brilliant with hospitality: warm, friendly, inviting.

When my mother had to go into the home, Maria stepped into my life in a big way. In effect, she became my surrogate mum. She and Alan introduced me to many new culinary delights, and generally became my new family. In truth, many of my Christian friends fit that bill, but there is something special about

Maria. When I had to have my faithful companion, my beautiful black Labrador, Timber, put to sleep, who was there with me? Maria. When I felt adrift at Christmas, who was there? Maria. I don't know what I'd have done without her, especially in the early days.

One of the dishes she has served me over the years, when I have dropped by to talk and to pray, is a very quick and easy pasta recipe. I was rather surprised to find out that the name 'Puttanesca' has a less than innocent meaning. Apparently this recipe, dating back to the mid-twentieth century, was used by the 'ladies of the night'. This made me think about Jesus and His encounter with the 'sinful woman' in Luke chapter 7. There, we see how the religious Pharisee has invited Jesus to dinner – but hasn't paid Him the common courtesy of a proper welcome. There is no love in his so-called 'hospitality'. The 'sinful woman', however, shows her gratitude in being forgiven by pouring perfume on the feet of Jesus. What a contrast! What a difference we see here between lavish love and cold-hearted judgement.

I'm glad I'm under grace and that my sins are forgiven. When we encounter Jesus, and realise that He loves us so much, that He wants relationship with us more than we want relationship with Him, that He pursues us, protects us, and guides us, it gives us a different perspective on life and people. He truly is the God of the second chance: the One who restores and blesses, as He did with me.

When Maria entertains, she is lavish in her love for people. She is also lavish in her love for God.

Puttanesca sauce reminds me that I'm part of a family. God's family. I'm not alone. Jesus loves me lavishly – after all, He provided Maria.

Puttanesca Sauce Serves 2

This sauce derives from the back streets of Naples. It is quick and tasty.

Ingredients

Your favourite pasta

Grated Parmigiano

Fresh basil

For the sauce:

2 tablespoons olive oil

2 cloves garlic, finely chopped

1 red chilli, seeded and finely chopped

2oz canned anchovies, drained

6oz pitted black olives, roughly chopped

1 tablespoon capers, rinsed and drained

500g tomato passata

Salt and pepper

Method

1. In a pan, boil water with a little salt and a tablespoon of oil – this will stop the pasta from sticking together.
2. While the water comes to the boil and the pasta cooks, in a heavy-based pan add the olive oil, garlic, chilli, anchovies, olives, capers, tomato passata and salt and pepper to taste.
3. Stir gently. Cook the sauce for no more than 15 minutes, by which time the pasta should be al dente. With tongs, take the pasta from the boiling water and add to the pan with the sauce.
4. Toss the pasta, coating thoroughly with sauce. Top with chopped basil and lots of grated Parmigiano.

Harnessing the power of a Sunday lunch

Hospitality, food and faith go hand in hand, and always did for me as I grew up. There is huge power in coming together at the table, sharing food and opening up to one another. I find there is no other setting where people feel so at ease and willing to share stories than at the dinner table over good food, which is why I am passionate in encouraging people to get together and eat. It never needs to be fussy or impressive, just simple food served graciously.

When I was growing up, Sundays were always a time my family prioritised for building friendships and community over a roast lunch. Shaping my view on hospitality, my parents always cooked for seven or eight people rather than just the four of us, so they could invite people back to eat with us after church. Students from the local university, families new to the area, widowed older ladies; all have pulled up a chair at our big pine table and joined our family for the afternoon. Very rarely would we ever eat a meal alone, and my mum always had ingenious tips up her sleeve for stretching food to feed however many people they opened the door to. I'd be in charge of dessert, so had the joyful task of throwing together mountainous piles of profiteroles or giant bowls of chocolate mousse to feed a crowd – always received by our guests with glee. This recipe for a lemon meringue profiterole pile is scrumptious, feeds a crowd and can be prepared ahead of time, which makes it perfect for those throw-together lunches.

Lemon Meringue Profiteroles

Ingredients

For the pastry:

75g butter, diced

1 teaspoon caster sugar

50g plain flour

50g strong bread flour

3 eggs

Filling:

250ml double cream

100g lemon curd

Zest of one lemon

Meringue topping:

2 egg whites

150g sugar

Express:
You can freeze the profiteroles before or after they have been filled. Empty shells will take 15 minutes to defrost, and filled shells will take 30 minutes. You can even eat them from frozen, as the lemon cream sets into a parfait centre.

Method

1. Preheat the oven to 180C/160C fan/gas mark 4. Line two large baking trays with parchment.

2. Place the butter, sugar and 125ml of water into a small saucepan over a medium-high heat. Bring the mixture to a rolling boil, and when all the butter has melted, add the flour and vigorously beat the mixture with a wooden spoon until a smooth ball of dough forms.

3. Keep the pan on the heat and continue to cook the dough for a further minute, stirring all the time. Tip the dough into a bowl and leave it to cool until it has stopped steaming. If the dough hasn't cooled properly when you add the eggs, they will scramble.

4. Beat the eggs together briefly in a small jug. Add the eggs into the cooled dough in 3 separate additions, beating well in between each one. It can be quite difficult to work in, but keep mixing and it will turn into a thick paste. Your mixture should fall off a spatula easily and leave a 'v' shape, so add the final amount slowly. You might not need to add all the egg. Spoon the choux pastry into a piping bag.

5. Pipe the dough into 2.5cm buns, leaving enough space between each one for it to expand. Use a wet finger to smooth over any points. Bake for 20-25 minutes or until golden brown and hollow, then turn off the oven and allow them to cool completely in the oven. This will dry out the pastry and avoid any soggy choux.

6. While the pastry is drying, make the lemon cream filling. Whip the cream into soft peaks in a large bowl, then fold through the lemon curd and lemon zest. Spoon into a piping bag and set to one side.

7. To make the meringue topping, place the sugar into a small saucepan with 75ml water. Heat the mixture on a medium heat, stirring until the sugar has dissolved. When the grains of sugar have dissolved, bring the mixture to the boil. Use a sugar thermometer to measure the temperature.

8. While the syrup is heating up, whisk the egg whites into soft peaks using a handheld electric whisk or in a stand mixer. When the sugar syrup reaches 118C, pour it gradually into the whites, whisking all the time. Continue to whisk the meringue for 10 minutes until it is really thick and glossy. Transfer the meringue into a piping bag so it is ready to use.

9. Pierce a small hole into the bottom of each cooled profiterole and fill with the lemon cream. Arrange about 10 profiteroles on a large serving plate as the bottom layer. Construct a pyramid, using a little meringue as glue.

10. Pipe the meringue mixture around the profiterole stack. Use a blowtorch to brown the meringue to get the full lemon meringue effect! Serve immediately.

Published with permission of HarperCollins, recipe taken from CRAVE by Martha Collison, photograph by Laura Edwards

This is my take on lemon meringue pie – choux style! Deliciously light pastry stuffed with zingy lemon cream, all enrobed in Italian meringue. Whenever my family host a spontaneous dinner party or family lunch, profiteroles are one of my go-to recipes. Choux pastry can be made really quickly, they bake and cool while we eat, and then can be filled and served in a matter of minutes. You can replace the lemon curd with any kind of curd – lime, orange or passion fruit all work really well.

Welcoming the outsider

Radical table fellowship

When you read of the Lord eating with 'sinners', what goes through your mind? The Lord tells the religious leaders why He ate with 'sinners' by saying, 'It is not the healthy who need a doctor, but those who are ill … I have not come to call the righteous, but sinners' (Matthew 9:12-13). His reasoning seems so concise and understandable that we may not give much more attention to the Lord's seemingly simple practice of eating with 'sinners' and miss its great significance.

In 2007, my reading of such texts radically changed when I visited India to study caste prejudice within the Indian Church and society. On my first evening I attended St George's Cathedral in Chennai, and at the end of the service introduced myself to the minister, who promptly invited me to an evening meal with his family. Towards the end of the meal he asked how I was getting home, and I said that the person who had driven me was waiting to take me. He replied, 'You should have invited him to join us, we could have enjoyed table fellowship with him.' I mumbled that I'd given him money to buy himself a meal as I realised that, within twenty-four hours of arriving to study caste prejudice in others, my very own caste bigotry had been laid bare. On the drive back, I stared out of the window as tears flowed at my abject failure.

The next morning someone else was driving and I was determined to make amends and practise table fellowship. I invited him to join me for breakfast at a restaurant, and my insistence eventually led him to accept. However, he would only have a coffee, and there was more of him hanging off the bench than was sitting on it. He looked nervous and very uncomfortable as the restaurant owner stared and, gulping down his coffee, my driver made a quick exit. Then I understood the cultural cues. I'd invited him to a restaurant frequented by those of a higher caste than him. The restaurant owner wasn't going to tell me, someone from the high-ranking Brahmin caste, not to bring this man in, but my guest knew he was somewhere above his caste 'station'. The next day I asked him to choose where we ate breakfast, and he gladly did so. Not only did he eat, he even ordered seconds! While I did not feel uncomfortable, I was aware of being the outsider and in an unfamiliar setting. Sadly, the driver changed the next day, so I could not develop a relationship to learn and share.

These experiences brought fresh perspective to my reading of the Lord eating with people the religious leaders called 'sinners'. How did the 'sinners' feel as the Pharisees fixed them with a hard stare of disapproval as they ate with the Lord? How did Matthew, Zacchaeus and other tax collectors feel as the religious leaders muttered and poured scorn on them as they feasted with the Lord and honoured Him? However they may have felt, the Lord gladly ate with them, honoured them, and brought salvation and peace to them. That His eating with 'sinners' caused such consternation for the Pharisees reveals that the Lord met and ate with them on a consistent basis, demonstrating true love, affirmation and acceptance, rather than engaging in a passing fad.

Crucially, when the Lord saw the fledgling faith of those on the religious margins, He encouraged and fanned it into flame, often by eating with them.

When the Lord boldly invited Himself to Zacchaeus' house, His honoured host was soon agreeing to give half his possessions to the poor and to make restitution to those he had cheated. As the Lord said, 'Today salvation has come to this house, because this man, too, is a son of Abraham. For the Son of Man came to seek and to save the lost' (Luke 19:9-10).

The Lord's radical table fellowship also extended beyond His immediate culture. In John 4, after conversing with the Samaritan woman, the Lord spent two days in the Samaritan town of Sychar. Though Jews do not associate with Samaritans and there was enmity between them, the Lord spent a considerable amount of time with these Samaritans, eating, drinking and forming relationships with them. While being clear about the gospel message, the Lord boldly broke religious, cultural and ethnic barriers through His practice of table fellowship – could the two things be meant to go hand in hand?

But what of His own? What of those who forsook Him in His darkest hour? Prior to the cross, the Lord's final meal was with His twelve disciples who would all abandon Him, Peter denying Him three times and Judas betraying Him to death. Yet through this gathering He instituted the new covenant meal, which we still observe today, ushering in a new community in which every barrier is broken and to which every 'failed' disciple is welcome. Whoever believes in Him is born again, reconciled to God and each other. All believers are welcome at the Lord's table. Shortly after His resurrection, on the shore of the Sea of Galilee, the Lord gave evidence of this as He became the host, inviting

His disciples to eat bread and charcoal-cooked fish with Him. After the meal, after acceptance had already been shown through fellowshipping over food, the Lord 'officially' reinstated Peter (John 21).

In short, the Lord ate with people who no religious leaders of His day, no respectable persons, would have done. With whom do you and I eat? Who do we invite to our dinner parties? The Lord taught, 'When you give a luncheon or dinner, do not invite your friends, your brothers ... if you do, they may invite you back and so you will be repaid. But when you give a banquet, invite the poor, the crippled, the lame, the blind, and you will be blessed. Although they cannot repay you, you will be repaid at the resurrection of the righteous' (Luke 14:12-14). While the Lord is not saying we should never invite family and friends to eat with us, is there a need to rebalance who we invite, and invite those on the margins of society into our spaces to share meals with us, invite those others prefer not to have at their table?

Such efforts need to be consistent and long term. Hospitality that is sporadic or that is offered to salve our conscience will be seen for what it is. The Lord exhibited consistent unconditional love and willingness to eat and fellowship with 'sinners'. Over time, tax collectors and 'sinners' would have realised the genuineness of His loving concern for them and His commitment to breaking the ungodly social and religious barriers that kept them at a distance.

> The Lord ... went to commune and fellowship personally with those ostracised and overlooked by the society of His day

Whether the Lord ever invited people to a home of His own in Nazareth or Capernaum may not be known, but it is absolutely clear that He went to the homes of diverse people to eat with them. He entered their spaces where they were comfortable, which is what I learned to do in India. Churches' efforts to run soup kitchens and night shelters, to support the vulnerable and lonely, are truly excellent examples of Christian love in action, although they usually involve people coming to us, and of course people are served on behalf of an organisation. But the Lord didn't just go to serve on behalf of a group – He went to commune and fellowship personally with those ostracised and overlooked by the society of His day. I have no answer here, but raise this question: where and how can we both serve and fellowship with those on the margins?

The Lord's behaviour raises a further challenge for us, because as He eats with others, He also receives honour. In one instance Matthew, His host, holds a banquet in His honour (Matthew 9:10), and on other occasions people other than His host honour Him at meals, as when He is anointed by a 'sinful' woman as He eats at the home of Simon the Pharisee (Luke 7:36-50), and when He is anointed with expensive perfume by a woman at the home of Simon the Leper in Bethany (Mark 14:3-9). While we are ready to host, give and serve in our homes, are we also prepared to be hosted, to receive and be served at others' tables? When people are given the chance to serve and honour us, they too are honoured and dignified as in accepting their hospitality we implicitly accept them.

The Lord's practice of table fellowship gives us a fresh perspective on God's desire for human well-being and flourishing. Through the simple yet vital necessity of sharing food, the Lord breaks every barrier and invites us to replicate His barrier-breaking practices. As a guest, He dignified those on the religious margins, challenging us to do likewise. And as a host, He served His broken disciple and poured the soothing balm of forgiveness upon Peter's troubled soul. As He invited Peter, so too He invites us to follow Him, to feed and be fed by His sheep, wherever they may be found.

Compelled to listen

Each week, a multi-ethnic, multifaith group of people from our community come together to prepare a community lunch at the Springfield Project, which is attached to St Christopher's Church in Springfield, Birmingham. It is a beautiful project in that in a community where most of us come from somewhere else and have varying amounts of English, food is a great equaliser. Different people take turns being in charge of the meal so that we learn from one another, and as we cook, we talk about our food, our culture, our families.

In such a multifaith community, faith conversations happen very naturally because most of us have a faith and are comfortable talking about it together. Because of our connection with The Feast Youth Project, we generally use the principles of The Feast's 'Guidelines for Dialogue' as a basis (see page 107 for more information). After we have eaten, people naturally go into the kitchen to help wash the dishes, which continues the companionable atmosphere. I think the general effect has been a real sense of belonging among the people who come.

On Maundy Thursday, we made hot cross buns and ma'amoul, an Arabic holiday biscuit eaten at Muslim, Jewish and Christian holidays in the Middle East. As we cooked, we compared our beliefs on Jesus' life and the events of Good Friday and Easter. When we are with people who believe the same thing, it is easy to be dismissive of the beliefs of others, but as we stood together rolling dough and pressing biscuits, we were compelled to listen and to try to understand each other. It takes time to work out how to love and respect one another while still longing for the other to believe as we do.

Here's to lots more weeks of cooking and talking together!

'He makes ...
wine that gladdens human hearts,
oil to make their faces shine,
and bread that sustains their hearts'

Psalm 104:14-15

Telling truth through food and story

As our local church in Sheffield moves deeper into cross-cultural mission, my husband, Blessan, together with a few other men from the church, has been hosting a weekly event aptly called Food and Story. It is an outreach to men from international backgrounds within the city, many of whom have become friends through connections with the local community or through refugee ministry. The event revolves around sharing a meal together and a story from the Bible. Each week the men are welcomed into one of our homes, where there is space and time for sharing life stories and challenges and offering prayer and support.

Sharing food together takes us on a journey into a deeper friendship. Receiving hospitality from other cultures is a way of enabling us to receive and to keep us humble. It also breaks down some of our cultural strongholds. You cannot hold on to your cultural pride, as around the table each one is eating in their own style; for example, some people eat with their hands, some people use a knife and fork, some chew on chicken bones, whereas others just nibble the white and brown meat and frown at the gristle. In this place of acceptance, the participants can enjoy the food without compromising their cultural identity. The non-judgemental atmosphere leads to some cultural prejudices being challenged without anything being directly said. This then enables each man to host themselves without feeling the pressure to maintain a particular standard.

Ultimately, it's not about food; it's all about sharing life. This creates a platform to share personal stories, both the triumphs and the trials. Each person's story becomes everyone's story. Everybody is part of God's bigger Story.

Waleed* was an Afghani asylum seeker who had lived in the Middle East most of his life. He had come to the UK under a lorry on the pretext that he was a Syrian, having been told that he was much more likely to get asylum in the UK if he was Syrian. His fictional story of capture by ISIS and brainwashing in an ISIS camp was bold and believable, despite its extremity, as we all know the atrocities that ISIS has committed.

Waleed was building a strong friendship and finding acceptance with the local church. At one of the Food and Story events, Waleed listened to the story about Jesus and His disciples on a boat in the storm and was amazed by the way that Jesus provided hope for the men. This story proved to be a light that Waleed could hold on to in the dark days to come, when he ended up being detained by the Home Office and moved from one detention centre to another in the UK. The love that he had experienced from the church members together with the stories he had been learning from the Bible convicted him of the need to tell the truth about his situation. One desperate day in December 2017, about to board a plane to the previous country in which he had sought asylum, Waleed told the authorities the truth about who he was and where he had come from and was released back into the asylum system with a new case.

This miraculous intervention was a sign to Waleed that God was for him, and it was all triggered by the sharing of food and stories. After coming back, he was brave enough to come and apologise to those of us who had heard his initial story for misleading us, and explained to us what had led to this decision. This was an indication of a genuine heart transformation.

Moru (Buttermilk) Curry Serves approximately 10

Moru is a standard accompaniment for any rice dish in Kerala and is often mixed with other curries.

Ingredients

500ml yogurt

Water (to form liquid consistency)

Salt and pepper to taste

½ teaspoon turmeric

Pinch cumin

½ teaspoon fenugreek

Small onion or shallot

1 inch ginger

2 cloves garlic

Handful curry leaves

2 teaspoons mustard seeds

Pinch chilli powder

Method

1. Scoop the yogurt into a saucepan and add water and salt. Mix till the yogurt is the consistency of a thin smoothie.

2. Add the turmeric and cumin and heat the curry slowly.

3. Crush the fenugreek to a powder and add it to the mix. Cook for around 10 minutes until the liquid steams. Don't let it boil or it will curdle.

4. In the meantime, cut up the onion, ginger and garlic cloves into thin slices and set aside with the curry leaves. Fry the mustard seeds in oil until the seeds crackle, then add the ingredients you set aside. Fry until the garlic browns slightly. Add the chilli powder.

5. Add the fried ingredients to the yogurt and stir.

* not his real name

Christmas kindnesses with foreigners and strangers

My dad came to England in the 1950s. My mum and my six-year-old sister arrived a few years after this and a year later I was born. The image of Indians in England back then was very much informed by the history of British colonialism. Most of the men from Gujarati farming villages worked in factories across England. They spoke little to no English and worked the hardest jobs for the lowest pay and struggled to purchase a home of their own. My family were one of the few Asian families in Tipton, West Midlands. We lived on a street of ten terraced houses.

Celebrations are generally a time when the separation from family and culture is felt the most by migrants. Christmas is definitely one of those times. Our family Christmases from the late 1960s to the 1980s continue to be among the most mentioned memories of many of my extended family and friends to this day.

We knew some of our neighbours well. Mr and Mrs McHugh of Slater Street will always be our favourites. Their sons, John and Richard, were much older than us, yet Mrs McHugh took it upon herself to include us in some of the cultural aspects of life in Britain. On the day before Christmas Eve, Mrs McHugh would arrange for us to have a turkey from her brother's farm. It came mostly plucked. My mum, my sisters and I pulled out the last stubborn quills and prepared the bird by rinsing it and making a contraption with wire coat hangers and string to hang the bird between two dining chairs to drain.

On Christmas Eve, my sisters and I would make sure our kitchen was spotless for the arrival of Mrs McHugh. There was a hush as she entered the kitchen with a big bowl of her home-made stuffing of pork and herbs; ingredients our mum never used but which evoked in us illusions of the exoticness of English cuisine. Mrs McHugh would put the stuffed turkey in the oven before her family left for Christmas Eve Mass at Sacred Heart Catholic Church.

On Christmas morning we would rush downstairs to a beautifully warm living room, with magical aromas wafting from the kitchen. We hurriedly bathed and put on our best clothes; hair gleaming with oil was tightly braided and tied off with new ribbons. We sat in a row on the blue settee waiting in eager anticipation for that knock on the door. That excitement in the room was the best feeling of my entire childhood! Mrs McHugh would enter and wish us all a Merry Christmas. In her arms she carried beautifully wrapped gifts for each of us. Knowing my love for reading, she gave me a new book every year. We did our best to not eagerly tear off the wrapping, but politely and graciously, as befitting our Eastern culture, we tried to wait until she had at least reached the front door. I'm sure she heard our squeals of delight as we opened our very first gifts.

Before leaving, she would go in the kitchen and check the turkey and let us know what time it would be ready to eat before returning to her home to finish meal preparations for her own family. For us, there were no side dishes of boiled vegetables. These were unpalatable to us back then. Instead, we had a dozen or more loaves of sliced white bread and made mounds of turkey sandwiches accompanied by traditional bhajia and other Indian food.

> Her behaviour was instrumental in our community's love and respect for Christian kindess, compassion and generosity

As the day continued, friends and family would arrive. Few if any Asians in the West Midlands had cars in the early years, neither were there buses running on Christmas Day. I remember hearing of one family that walked several miles to our house to share Christmas with us. Throughout the day the steady stream of visitors would ask news of Mrs McHugh's family, having become familiar with her annual generosity.

Christmases like these continued through my teens. One spring we moved to West Bromwich where we ran a corner shop. Around Christmas of that year, my dad drove to Slater Street to deliver a gift, only to discover that Mrs McHugh had passed away a few days earlier. I still shed a tear remembering how much she had touched an entire community with her kindness. Her behaviour was instrumental in our community's love and respect for Christian kindness, compassion and generosity.

To this day, wherever in the world my family celebrates anything, we make a point of welcoming the foreigner and the stranger, as we were also once foreigners and strangers in the land.

'For I was hungry and you gave me something to eat, I was thirsty and you gave me something to drink, I was a stranger and you invited me in'

Matthew 25:35

A café that connects

In the summer of 2014, a vitally important and unique event was started in Gloucester, one which reflects the multicultural wealth of our city. The World Café is built around a community meal, cooked by people who have often recently arrived in the city and want to engage with local people and learn about the culture, but mostly want to feel free simply to be themselves and share their own cultural riches. The World Café is a place where lives are shared, where we are all interconnected. It is a place where people who can be struggling to adapt to their new home can thrive and find fulfilment by being with others.

A meal is a big part of it. It is the glue that brings us together, helping local people to welcome strangers into their city, strangers who have suffered war, lost family, been orphaned, widowed, suffered persecution because of their faith, lost land, homes, jobs, and are sometimes even so traumatised that they have lost the ability to speak. They are strangers in a strange place, the often hidden community of refugees, asylum seekers and migrants among us.

Having come from Lithuania, together with my husband, to work as a missionary in the UK, the work of the café is very close to our hearts because we know what it is to be strangers in a strange land. The World Café vision is to follow Christ's steps, 'For I was hungry and you gave me something to eat, I was thirsty and you gave me something to drink, I was a stranger and you invited me in, I needed clothes and you clothed me, I was ill and you looked after me, I was in prison and you came to visit me' (Matthew 25:35-36). These words are not just beautiful; they also demonstrate what it means to be truly human, what it means to share a meal with a stranger, what it means to care for someone who has lost everything, what it means to share life.

When we sit around the table we share not only food, but also suffering. Life is full of pain, as we know. And when we share suffering and help one another come out on the other side, we rejoice together. And the joy is real with praise and thanks.

Thus we give a special welcome to all refugees and asylum seekers living in the city. Sharing a meal together is the focus of the World Café, where the food does not just feed our physical bodies, but it also helps us to overcome our cultural, ethnic and religious prejudices. Thus, the hospitality expressed through food becomes a bridge between physical and spiritual hunger. After all, as human beings we have two things in common – food and suffering. The World Café is a place where strangers can become friends and encourage and care for one another.

The way of love

was contacted by a refugee charity and asked if I could host a Kurdish couple who in the midst of their asylum claim process had found themselves locked out of their attic flat as the Home Office had stopped paying for the rent. The solicitor would prepare an emergency court case to challenge this decision, but in the meantime, they were homeless. So I picked up two strangers on whose faces I could read the stress they had been under. In a foreign land, not having mastered the language yet, confused by the randomness of the Home Office decision and completely dislocated – once again. They stayed at my home for three weeks.

Being an immigrant myself, I remembered how difficult it is to leave home. I was moved by their account and had respect for their resilience. It was a joy to accompany them to some appointments at the bank or the GP. We enjoyed a concert by a Syrian refugee orchestra. Their faces beamed when they heard familiar music and saw the wonderful ethnic mix of the audience. Some of the older Syrian men danced in the aisles. We all stood and cheered them on. When the first violinist said, 'In moments like this I feel at home', the Kurdish couple nodded in agreement.

Preparing food also made them feel at home. On many a day I would come home and the table had been set. I ate some lovely dishes and was introduced to new tastes. And they enjoyed my Dutch lentil dish too! At dinner we would talk about our day. We would Google what we couldn't put into words and laugh about the tricky English language. We would talk about our families back home and wonder about the days ahead. These were simple meals, yet rich. Unforgettable, in fact.

I invited them to church. They loved it. The kindness of people who were strangers to them spoke louder than words. A good thing too, as language was still a barrier. In fact, from the moment they arrived in the UK they found themselves bumping into the people of God: the foodbank run by a church; the English language class facilitated by a Christian; a place to stay at my home ... The hospitality they enjoyed seemed to be the way of Jesus.

Back in their home village they had seen the Jesus film in a home cinema and it had made them cry. Here in a new land, the followers of Christ were providing them with a bed, bath and bread. Hospitality creating a place of refuge; Christians reweaving society in which such huge gaps emerge. Love, said American bishop Michael Curry at Harry and Meghan's wedding, is a dynamic power to heal the world: 'When love is the way, the earth will be a sanctuary.' Love creates a new human family.

'God sets the lonely in families', the psalmist says in Psalm 68:6. And indeed, we were a proper little household. In God's house there are 'many rooms' (John 14:2). And in my house there is one spare room. Throughout our life we enjoy the benefits of the Father's household and we can bring honour to Him by the way we live – by the way we love.

During the Sunday service, we prayed for justice to be done. Our prayer was heard when a fortnight later the judge addressed the injustice and ordered the UK government to continue to provide accommodation for them until the asylum procedure was completed. On Friday afternoon we said goodbye. A Bible in their own language was now a much-valued addition to their meagre belongings. I gave them the address of a church in their new home town. On Sunday morning they texted me a selfie: 'Hi, Marijke, your friends at church, they're very welcome.'

The way of love continues.

Dutch Lentil Bake Serves 4

Ingredients

350g green lentils

3 eggs

1 small tub double cream

150g grated cheese

1 finely cut onion

1 small tin sweetcorn

100g cashew nuts

Salt, pepper, nutmeg

Salad ingredients of your choice

Method

1. Cook green lentils in a pan with water for about 30 minutes until lentils are soft.

2. Drain the water and put lentils in a bowl.

3. Add the eggs, double cream, grated cheese, finely cut onion, sweetcorn and cashew nuts to the lentils.

4. Season with salt, pepper and nutmeg.

5. Place in an oven dish at 200C/180C fan/gas mark 6 for 20 minutes.

6. Serve with salad.

'Freely you have received;
freely give'

Matthew 10:8

Sharing the director's table

Poulet DG is a Cameroonian dish. It is a chicken stew cooked in aromatic flavours (herbs and spices), served with a cocktail of fried banana plantains and vegetables (carrots, peppers, green beans). It's a simple recipe that requires only a few exotic ingredients.

This dish dates from the 1980s and comes from the Bamileke tribe (in the western region of Cameroon).

Poulet is the French word for chicken. DG is the acronym for Directeur Général in French, which means managing director or CEO. The recipe is called Poulet DG because it was traditionally only served to the upper class in Cameroon. This was because it contained ingredients such as chicken and plantain which weren't eaten every day and were relatively expensive.

However, today it is a dish that is eaten among all the classes. It has become very popular in western Cameroon because it is very tasty and the ingredients are easy to find and accessible to all. I believe eating good food together should not exclude anyone, regardless of class or profession, and so this is a good example of how a dish that used to be reserved for just the elite is now enjoyed by anyone and everyone.

Banana plantains and chicken have always been my favourite dishes. When I was asked by a friend to cook a Cameroonian dish for a Christian fellowship meeting to introduce others to some of my culture, it was a simple decision to cook Poulet DG. Unlike some other Cameroonian recipes, Poulet DG ingredients are easy to get in London. The recipe is straightforward and always turns out well. I like to serve it with fried rice; it's a great way to start off a time of fellowship as it always seems to bring people together!

Poulet DG Serves 6

Ingredients

6 large ripe plantains (neither too soft nor too hard)

1 whole chicken (5lb or 2.5kg)

1 large onion, finely chopped

1 sliced leek

¼ each of 4 coloured bell peppers, chopped

2 large carrots, cut into slices

4 cloves garlic, minced

1 teaspoon salt

½ teaspoon ground pepper

½ teaspoon ground ginger

1 habanero (hot) pepper or paprika – optional

5 large tomatoes, cut into cubes

300g green beans, cut and blanched

Method

1. Heat vegetable oil in a pan. Peel the plantains and cut them into slices.

2. Fry the plantains on both sides and set them aside.

3. Cut the chicken into pieces. Salt and pepper then put it in a saucepan.

4. Cook the chicken for 15 minutes on a medium-high heat in a large volume of water – when finished, keep a little of the water for step 8.

5. Fry the cooked chicken in a pan on both sides – or bake it in the oven at 200C/180C fan/gas mark 6 for 15 minutes (until it reaches a golden brown colour).

6. In the same pan in which you fried the plantains, take away more than half of the oil and cook the onion, leek, bell peppers and carrots. Add the garlic, salt, pepper and ground ginger, and the habanero pepper or paprika if desired.

7. Add the tomatoes, stir and leave on a medium heat for about 2 minutes.

8. Add the chicken with the water kept from step 4, cover and simmer for 15 minutes.

9. Add the fried plantains and green beans, and stir. Cover and let the flavours blend for about 5 minutes and your dish is ready to serve.

10. Make sure chicken is cooked through before serving (pierce with a fork and check there are no bloody juices close to the bone).

11. Serve hot. Enjoy it with a glass of juice or wine because this meal is just too special!

'They broke bread in their homes and ate together with glad and sincere hearts'

Acts 2:46

'Can we pray for you?'

It wasn't easy for her to walk through the door, but finances were tight and she didn't have anywhere else to go. The church foodbank was the only source of support that week so, with many questions about what she might find flowing through her mind, she took a breath and wandered in.

She was pleasantly surprised. 'I've never been received and welcomed in such a loving way,' she remarked. A group of Christians, being generous with their time and their food, made an impression on this Muslim woman in the midst of a difficult time.

The visit wasn't a one-off event. Life continued to be hard and the foodbank continued to provide. She got to know the staff a bit. Little by little the casual greetings led to some deeper talk. After some months, one of the Christians invited her to dinner with their family and friends. The food was plentiful and it was her joy to help clear up at the end. She wouldn't have had it any other way.

It was then an unexpected request was posed: 'Can we pray for you?'

Without delay the tears began to flow. Her marriage had fallen apart. Other memories burdened her in various ways. She didn't hesitate to agree, though. Her hosts prayed and she was reminded once again of their countercultural care.

That Christmas it was easy to say 'Yes' to festive events. While still unconvinced by the gospel, she knows beyond any shadow of doubt that Christians love. One day, we pray, she will join us in the heavenly feast as well …

Empowered through baking

Having fled a violent relationship, Nadia, nineteen, was living in a women's refuge with her one-year-old baby. She had a temporary roof over her head, but almost nothing else. Nadia's confidence was in pieces, and she didn't know how she would ever start to build a life for herself and her daughter.

That's when she met Luminary Bakery.

Here at Luminary, we were able to offer her a place on our training programme, designed to support the UK's most disadvantaged women in reaching their potential. Nadia arrived at our bakery on the first day, very nervous, but open-minded to see what she could learn. She loved food, and she loved to bake, but hadn't had the opportunity to do so in the past few years as she'd simply been surviving. Finally, at Luminary, she was able to take some time to invest in her own well-being and do something she really loved.

And Nadia isn't the only one. For many women at Luminary Bakery, being able to spend time learning, creating and investing in their own future is a luxury. We teach baking skills, from basic tips like how to use measuring scales, to complex techniques such as baking Danish pastry. Every week the trainees not only go away with products they have created themselves from scratch, but they've also spent a day with other women who have had similar experiences, sharing life together and being inspired that their future could look different.

We believe women are more than their past or current circumstances. They may have been exploited in the sex industry, be homeless, or have criminal convictions, but to us they are bakers. We don't ask that they disclose anything about their past unless they want to, as we want them to have the chance to define themselves by something new.

In the Bible, there are many instances of people being given a new name to mark a new way of living; words have significance. Becoming 'bakers', discovering this new identity and finding a supportive community of other women can be completely transformative. Women who have previously been defined by their disadvantage are now instead defined by their potential.

We believe all people are created equal, with equal value, and we love demonstrating that by empowering women to believe in their own worth. Likewise, we believe that gaining employment has real significance, not only because being able to provide for yourself is liberating, but also because working can create a sense of purpose and identity.

Luminary was set up in response to God's prompting to address the injustice we saw in our city. And it exists so that women can be empowered to change their circumstances, through the art and skill of baking. We've chosen to combine the therapeutic mindfulness of baking with professional career options in the hospitality industry, so that women like Nadia now have the chance to build a future for themselves and their families. The healing found in creating delicious food for others to enjoy gives these women identity, connects them back into community and gives them the chance to live life to the full.

Luminary Bakery's Courgette, Cheddar and Black Pepper Soda Bread

Usually still warm from the oven, we sell loaves of our fresh soda bread from our neighbourhood café in Stoke Newington every day. Customers often comment they can smell it cooking from down the street! It's a quick bread, meaning exactly that: with no kneading or proving time, it's very quick to make. This bread is always best eaten on the day it's made, but makes great toast too, especially when slathered in some salted butter.

Makes 1 large loaf

Ingredients

250g wholemeal flour

250g plain white flour, plus a handful for dusting

1 teaspoon bicarbonate of soda

1 teaspoon salt

1 teaspoon freshly cracked black pepper, plus a little for the top

200g mature cheddar, grated

1 teaspoon English mustard

200g courgette, grated

350g buttermilk (or you can make your own from 250g natural yogurt + 100g milk)

Method

1. Preheat your oven to 200C/180C fan/gas mark 6.

2. In a large bowl, mix together the two types of flour, bicarbonate of soda, salt, black pepper and grated cheese.

3. Mix the English mustard and grated courgette into the buttermilk.

4. Make a 'well' in the middle of the dry ingredients and pour the buttermilk into it. Using a spoon, and then your hands, mix in the buttermilk until a sticky dough forms.

5. Lightly dust your work surface with flour and tip the dough onto it.

6. Gently roll and fold the dough a couple of times to bring the mixture together, but do not knead.

7. Shape the dough into a ball. Using your hands, gently flatten the ball to about 1 inch thick and liberally dust with flour and black pepper.

8. Using a sharp knife, score the ball of dough with a deep cross, cutting 2/3 through and dividing it into quarters.

9. Place onto a baking tray lined with baking parchment and bake for 35-40 minutes. The loaf should be golden brown and oozing molten cheese once cooked.

10. Leave to cool on a wire rack. This is best eaten on the day of baking and makes great toast for days afterwards.

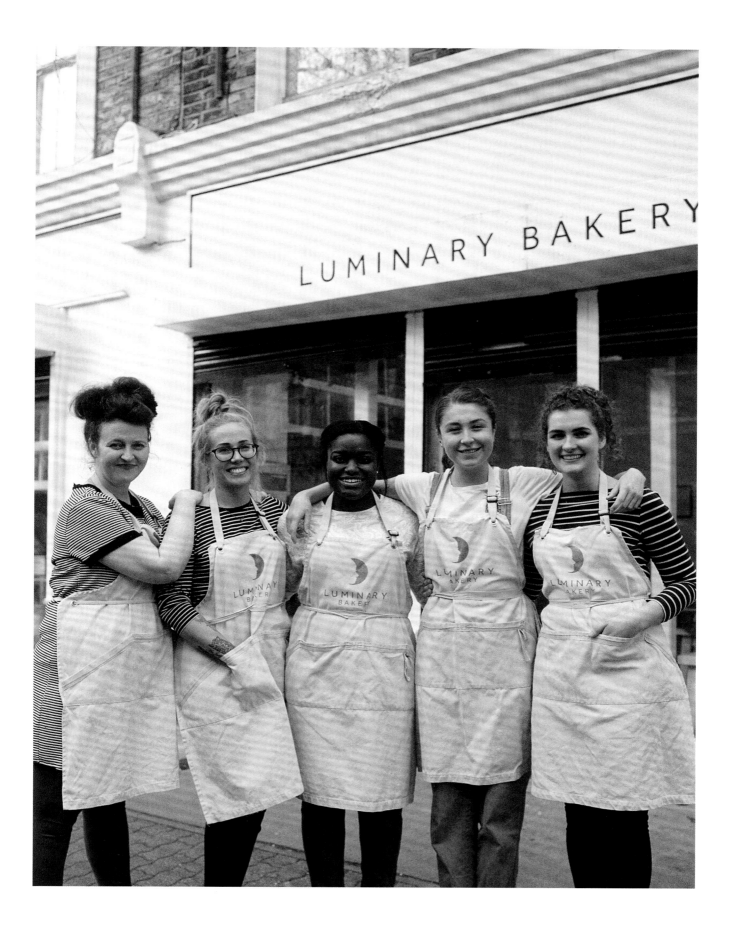

The Church of the Table

The Church of the Table began almost by accident some years ago when I was working in Modena, Italy. As a parish priest, every single day I had homeless people and migrants in need coming to my door asking for money. I often asked myself: what would be the best way of helping them?

I was convinced that to give money was a trap. It would turn our relationship into a transactional arrangement: I would be washing my hands of their problems by handing over some coins. And it wouldn't solve the real problems of the people. So what should I do?

I decided to invite these people into my home. We would chat together, share stories and I hoped I would begin to understand their needs better. Then one day, lunchtime arrived and I decided to invite them to stay and share a meal. We then continued to have lunch together over the following days. We would cook pasta with butter and parmesan, together with whatever ingredients we had to hand – tomatoes, greens, meat – whatever people gave us.

That was ten years ago and every day since, anybody who wishes has come for lunch: anyone can knock at the door. But it is not a canteen – we say it is a 'family table'. People are considered our friends and guests, not 'customers' or 'users'.

The difference is everyone helps in the making of the meal and clearing up, just like in a family, so each person is useful and valued, which is especially important for people who have been excluded for a long time from normal family life. This is a Common Good approach where each person takes responsibility; each of us is needed.

Coming together over food around a table has a healing power for everyone: lonely people find friends and companionship; the suffering find consolation;

the angry find mercy and peace. Jesus did this many times. The real hunger of many people concerns love rather than food. We aim to provide both.

And the benefits are mutual. I have gained so much. They've been teachers of life to me. Just by spending time together and through our conversations about loyalty, hospitality, faith and justice I have learned from their wisdom. Oh, and we pray together and laugh a lot.

While I now serve as a priest in Manila, the daily lunch continues back home thanks to volunteers, many of whom are themselves migrants. Every day, ten to twenty homeless and marginalised men and women, from different nations and religions, gather at the Church of the Table not only for a meal, but also to be transformed as they play their part and find family.

Spaghetti Aglio, Olio e Peperoncino
(Garlic, Oil and Chilli Pepper Spaghetti) Serves 5

Very, very simple but at the same time a traditional and delicious recipe! Because of the few ingredients, their quality is important.

Ingredients

500g or 700g Italian spaghetti (pasta di grano duro), the size that you prefer

5 cloves (fresh) garlic

30ml Italian extra virgin olive oil

Dried crushed hot chilli pepper, as much as you like

A cup fine, grated dried bread

Salt (both fine and coarse)

A cup grated aged cheese (optional)

Note: Big colanders for pasta are very helpful and simple to use. Professional cooks prefer to use handling colanders, pulling out pasta directly from the pot to the pan, a little at a time. This saves the boiling water: a useful element for the kitchen. Anyway, when you drain pasta, mix it immediately with the oil, or it'll stick quickly.

Method

1. Fill ¾ of a big pot with water, cover and put on the stove to boil.

2. Meanwhile, peel the garlic, cut it lengthwise into four parts.

3. Put the garlic with (about) 30ml of olive oil in a large cooking pan, put on a low heat and keep it gently mixed till the garlic becomes golden.

4. Add the desired quantity of chilli pepper.

5. Mix for another minute and turn off the stove.

6. When the water is boiling, put a ½ fist of coarse salt into the pot, then all the spaghetti. Mix and separate spaghetti immediately you put it in the water, before it sticks together; depending on the size of the pot, you can also break all the spaghetti in half before putting in. It is important that all the spaghetti is immersed in the boiling water.

7. Remove spaghetti from the boiling water, depending on your taste. In Italy the so-called pasta al dente is the most common cooking model: you should pull pasta off the stove just before it becomes soft. Cook's tip: To better impregnate the pasta with the flavouring and to conclude the cooking process, you have to put the pasta (well-drained) into the large pan of cooked oil with garlic and chilli pepper. On a low heat, mix well.

8. You can add some boiled water (no cold water!) if pasta is too dense to be easily mixed (but, remember, you are not preparing a soup); you can add some other crude olive oil if pasta seems too little flavoured (crude olive oil maintains its healthy properties and fragrance). You may also add some fine, grated dried bread, if you want to enrich the flavour. This gives a bit more density (the bread helps the pasta to better hold the flavouring). You can add more chilli pepper, but it is better to keep a low/medium hotness (it can be added later, individually).

9. Add cheese; it can be put on top, when spaghetti is in the dish.

Apart from the specific dish called 'pasta fredda', in Italy pasta is served immediately after its preparation, to keep the best flavour, and to aid digestion. Regarding the choice of the cheese, an aged local cheese is better than parmesan. Aged pecorino cheese is very good for this kind of pasta!

Nourishing community

Eating justly

When we talk about 'fellowship through food', we're usually referencing the shared experience of eating around a table with our families and immediate communities. This is a meaningful form of fellowship – many faith conversations are worked out in close relationships in the sacred space around the dinner table. However, there is another dimension of food fellowship which needs consideration: that of the people who supply our food – from grower to grocer.

In the UK, our plates are often filled from the far corners of the globe. Take, for example, a typical breakfast in my household: first, granola from the Austrian mountains goes in the bowl. Milk, proudly sourced from Welsh dairies, is poured next. Then, blueberries grown in Romania's warm continental climate are added. Bananas, harvested in Colombia while still green, then shipped on refrigerated 'reefers', get sliced and piled on. Finally, rich Manuka honey from remote parts of New Zealand gets drizzled over the top. Coffee, grown in Guatemala and roasted by our friends in Paisley, rounds off our breakfast.

Each of these ingredients goes through a range of inspections and can travel thousands of miles before it reaches our local grocer's shelf, being touched by many hands along the way. But when I stumble into the kitchen looking for breakfast early on a Monday morning, I often spare little thought for the people involved in the journey my food has taken to my refrigerator or fruit bowl. To the contemporary eater, to quote Wendell Berry's essay 'The Pleasures of Eating' in *What Are People For?*, 'food is pretty much an abstract idea – something they do not know or imagine – until it appears on the grocery shelf or on the table'.

A globalised market might not be inherently bad, but when food is grown or raised at such a distance from where it is consumed, it becomes easy to take its production for granted. The effect that consumption has on the supplier – for good or for bad – becomes theoretical at best. 'Rainforest certified' can mean very little when the only rainforest the consumer has ever seen was in a nature documentary. It should not be surprising that consumers feel detached from farmers, when the supermarket (or the delivery truck) is the only point of connection between the customer and the food industry.

However, even when it happens on another continent, our grocery shopping habits directly influence how our food is produced. When the 'best' purchase becomes the cheapest, or the biggest, or the nicest-looking, these factors drive the market. Thousands of tons of tasty, nutrition-filled produce go to waste every year because they do not fit industry standards for size, shape or colour. This wasteful practice can be devastating to small-scale farmers, whose produce cannot compete proportionally with industrial-sized farms. Additionally, producing big, shiny fruit and veg can require a great deal of chemical intervention, in the form of pesticides and fertilisers.

These chemicals can be harmful to the labourers who handle the food in the fields, as well as to local ecosystems. When our only point of reference is the finished product in our fruit bowl, it becomes easy to lose sight of the impact of the processes that brought it there.

In ancient Israel, this would have been a different story. What wasn't grown by a family would be purchased from farmers much closer to home. The Israelites would have known exactly where their food came from, and would likely have personally known each of the people involved in the process. Furthermore, the system by which Israelite families produced their food was regulated in the Torah. The entire agricultural system, from the division of land to the planting of crops, to the treatment and payment of workers, to the reaping and distribution of the harvest, and finally to the preparation and consumption of the final product, were all managed by a system of Old Testament laws (for example: Joshua 18:3-28; Deuteronomy 22:9; Leviticus 19:13; Leviticus 19:9-10; Exodus 12:43-49).

It is not enough, nor would it be prudent, to attempt to apply these Old Testament laws to twenty-first-century life as they were written. The original Israelite code, written during the Exodus, was intended for a society of fewer than a million people living in camps in the wilderness and in agrarian settlements. To take laws written for this ancient cultural setting and apply them directly to a post-industrial Western nation does not make sense. Giving a hired worker back his cloak before nightfall matters little in a society with central heating (Deuteronomy 24:13). As a result, the temptation seems to be to glaze over the Old Testament laws concerning economic systems as outdated and unimportant. However, to do this is to miss out on important writings which reveal the character of God.

> Our shopping habits, and how we feed ourselves and our families, should reflect the values of our faith

In *Sabbath as Resistance*, Walter Brueggemann argues that 'the God of Sinai who gives the Ten Commandments is never simply a "religious figure" but is always preoccupied with and attentive to socioeconomic practice and policy'. God is a God of justice and provision, distinctly concerned with the economy and day-to-day practices of the Israelites. Therefore, the economic systems and mundane practices through which a society sustains itself are incredibly spiritual matters. The God who is concerned with daily bread is of course concerned with how the baker earns a living.

If this was true of the ancient Israelites, then surely it is still true today. Our shopping habits, and how we feed ourselves and our families, should reflect the values of our faith. We may not leave fallow margins in our fields for the poor to glean, but we can certainly glean the edges of our cupboards for our local foodbanks (Leviticus 19:9; 23:22). We may not be directly hiring hands to harvest our crops, but their wages come out of what we pay at the till (Leviticus 19:13). While all of modern life might not grind to a halt to celebrate a year of jubilee, surely our land still cries out for Sabbath rest from the year-round cycle of planting and harvest required to bring us ripe fruit in the dead of winter (Leviticus 25).

Our call to fellowship starts at the table, but it does not end there. When we share food, we also share in a larger community, one which deserves consideration and care as well. Our responsibility to 'act justly' extends to the people who put food on our tables, at all stages in the process (Micah 6:8).

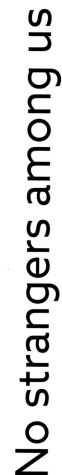

No strangers among us

When we started our new congregation three years ago, the question we were asking ourselves was: who are we to think we can build a church?

All we did was to apply the lessons we had learned in our ministry with international students. We determined to provide each week four things: 1) accessible biblical teaching without jargon, 2) practical application of Scripture, 3) simple modern worship and 4) consistent community expressed in eating a hot meal together each week.

Being a couple from two cultures (Peter is English, Lynette is from Singapore), we were prepared for the fact that many of our culturally English folk would struggle with the idea of supplying and eating dinner together every week. But we also knew that our Asian, African, South American and Caribbean brothers and sisters would be delighted and only too happy to pitch in and even showcase their national dishes.

We bought a chalkboard and wrote, 'On tonight's menu we have ...' giving not only the talk title and passage but the main course and dessert, too.

A church became a family party almost overnight. Parents who worried about their little ones' bedtimes soon accepted their offsprings' cries of, 'Can we stay for dinner?' Older members of the congregation got used to eating rice most weeks and developed a taste for curries and other Asian delights.

Having a single, long table ensured everyone – from the leadership to the newest visitor and the smallest child – was treated equally. We are still small – forty on a good day – but we are truly international.

Dinnertime talk is not always spiritual and more often it is just plain fun. We have come to know each other and discipleship happens in that context because church is no longer a spectator activity.

That may seem a lot to claim just because we eat together regularly; we cannot point to great numbers or successful evangelistic strategies. But we can say this: there simply are no strangers among us.

Baked Chicken Drumsticks Serves 40

Ingredients

Chicken drumsticks* (allow 2 per person plus a few extra)

8 tablespoons honey

8 tablespoons tomato sauce

6 tablespoons dark soy sauce

4 cloves garlic, finely chopped

A few splashes lemon juice

Salt and pepper, to taste

6 each peppers, mushrooms, carrots, finely sliced

Spring onions, finely chopped, for garnish

Method

1. Preheat oven to 220C/200C fan/gas mark 7. Slash drumsticks twice to allow to cook evenly.

2. Mix honey, tomato sauce, soy sauce, garlic and lemon juice in a bowl, adjusting amounts to taste. Add salt and pepper if needed.

3. Cover drumsticks with the mixed sauces and leave for at least 30 minutes (if possible, marinade earlier and leave aside for a few hours for flavour to develop).

4. Arrange peppers, mushrooms and carrots on a baking tray and arrange the drumsticks in a single layer on top (you may need more than one baking tray). Pour the leftover marinade on top. Place in preheated oven and cook at 220C/200C fan/gas mark 7 for 20 minutes.

5. Lower heat to 180C/160C fan/gas mark 4, turn drumsticks over and cook for a further 1 hour. Turn occasionally to ensure they cook evenly. If the mixture gets dry, add a little water or chicken stock.

6. Make sure chicken is cooked through before serving (pierce with a fork and check there are no bloody juices close to the bone).

7. For more gravy, use gravy mix with the cooking juices added in.

8. Sprinkle with spring onions. Serve with jasmine rice and mixed veg.

* Vegetarians: Reserve some of the vegetables before cooking, stir fry with sliced onion and add some of the honey, tomato sauce and soy sauce marinade. Bring to the boil. Add a little gravy mix to thicken. Pan fry Quorn fillet and add sauce. Serve hot.

'Anyone who welcomes you welcomes me, and anyone who welcomes me welcomes the one who sent me'

Matthew 10:40

The china tea set

I inherited a china tea set from my maternal grandmother. It is a complete set for twelve, green with pink roses and gold edging. Ornate, over the top and glorious. From my paternal grandmother I inherited, because nobody else wanted it, a silver-plated teapot, hot-water jug, sugar caddy and milk jug. The teapot is somewhat dented, but whenever I look at it I am transported back to sitting in, what was to a child, her endless lounge crowned with a blazing fire. The tea and toasted teacakes would arrive and she 'became Mum' and served the tea. She used to take great pride in every teacup having the same strength of tea and used her hot-water jug to perfection. This was a present given to her in 1924 from the Women's Guild in Cornwall on the occasion of her marriage. I love it, dents and all.

But why do I like the dents? Like everybody, I have experienced my share of hurt, difficulty, grief, disappointment, heartbreak. We all live with pain; however, every situation has proved the faithfulness of God – each 'dent' reminds me of how gracious He has been. I could wax lyrical for hours about my God, and the question I ask myself, in the light of His goodness, is: what can I share or give away in response to His kindnesses to me?

Jesus showed us how much He liked people, how He loved to be around them, and eating together was central. Every day we eat, so eating together – giving away by sharing – whenever possible is a no-brainer. Over the last forty years, my husband Steve and I have invited many people needing a place to live to come and join our family. Both we and our children derived enormous benefit from the many different cultures and experiences each brought into our home. With children, regular eating is mandatory, so the pattern developed that I would cook, and if our extended household joined us (their work allowing), we would all eat together. We lived on a tight budget; the food was basic but wholesome.

I am not a great cook. Honestly. And I'm not interested in producing anything 'gourmet'. I would rather watch programmes about buying and doing up houses than creating food! I like to keep things simple, but within that create an engaging experience for my guests. My interest centres on vegetables because I love them, and I am always excited to find a new way to cook an old favourite.

When Steve and I pondered how to facilitate bringing Christian leaders together, including those from different ethnic backgrounds, it became obvious it should be around food and drink. Here I paused. If I cooked an evening meal, besides being a huge undertaking for me if I did several courses, there was the problem of alcohol. Some Christians drink; others do not. Would we offend some, make fellowship difficult and miss out on their company?

Historically, we have done breakfasts. We opened our house to a Saturday Breakfast Club for years which ran from 9.30am till midday, depending on who kept hanging around. It worked a treat and continued for many years until we left Cobham in Surrey and moved to west London. A continental-type breakfast is an easy meal. We encouraged people to bring things to contribute. If you are a tentative host on a budget, I recommend this.

People do appreciate having a meal cooked for them, but it's the friendship they love. One thing I almost always do is pray over my food when I am cooking for others. I believe I have a secret ingredient available to everybody – the Holy Spirit! His presence in us and in our household transforms every experience. If people go away replete and happy, I thank the Holy Spirit for His help and beautiful presence. And I'm not being super-spiritual.

I had an idea: why not invite our fabulous leaders for afternoon tea? Everybody likes cake, and I decided even my limited skills could manage lovely sandwiches alongside scones, clotted cream and jam. It was also quintessentially English. Serving diverse teas or fruit juice would mean the whole question of alcohol would never occur, with fresh fruit, perhaps a bowl of strawberries and other non-dairy treats catering somewhat for allergies.

People do appreciate having a meal cooked for them, but it's the friendship they love

For an afternoon tea I knew I would not cope with the stress of having to make a lovely cake as a centrepiece. Play to your strengths, I always say! A friend makes cakes as a business so every time I hold a Garden Party I buy a superb, large carrot cake from her and everybody asks me if it's home-made. It is delicious and irresistible. There is also one hugely generous leader who, when she comes, never fails to bring a magnificent cake topped with yummy fruit.

Our annual Garden Party began eight years ago. It has been a joy to meet leaders, their spouses, even the occasional child, from the large evangelical spectrum of ethnicity we are graced with in this country. I love watching different people connect with each other, and connecting with them myself.

My maternal grandmother married Tom Horabin, who was a Liberal MP for North Cornwall 1939-1950. She put her china tea set to great use in their flat in London, hosting the movers and shakers of the political world. Entrusted with it and the teapot, I feel a sense of pride as their use continues, and I am reminded of God's faithfulness to me and His Church every time.

Opening our homes, meeting friends old and new at the door and reassuring them how pleased we are they have come, offering refreshment, will never date. It flows out of gratitude to God, and it is a privilege to give like Him.

'Do not forget to show hospitality to strangers, for by so doing some people have shown hospitality to angels without knowing it'

Hebrews 13:2

Out and about

Napoleon allegedly said that an army marches on its stomach. I've found that adage is true; for any group of people setting out for the day, the longer the route the more sustenance needed.

What happens when a group of young adults, passionate about the outdoors but living in central London, take adventure in one hand and hospitality in the other and use it to reach out to their friends?

Over the last few years, together with a group of friends at church, we have sought to combine our passion for outdoor pursuits with a desire to build and draw together a community that reflects God's love and shows His purpose in our lives.

On the weekends, this might look like a trip out of London to the surrounding counties and rolling hills, perhaps even a clifftop walk in Sussex or Kent. There is nothing quite like the exhausted feeling of satisfaction that accompanies reaching the end of a walk – perhaps only the looks of joy when you pull out a batch of home-made mint chocolate brownies or granola bars to replace the spent calories.

But the real adventure comes once a year when we take more time out from the capital – whether to Scotland, the Lake District, the Yorkshire Dales or Snowdonia, all destinations over the last few years for a longer break – and undertake a few walks that test our muscles and our psychological resolve. We keep on keeping on, and the moment we approach a summit, the competitive spirit wins out, and at least a few summon the last ounces of strength and will to race to the top.

Strong friendships are forged on the mountains; it's been a place where 'the ins and outs' of church community break down and friendships form. It provides a place where you cannot hide who you are, your weaknesses on show and your passion overflowing. We all need food on days like these – I know the cost when I've pushed to get over the next summit before calling a break, and the rebellion it has caused!

It's a time and place where I've found it easiest to talk about what matters most – except on the tough stretches when silence ensues and each breath is carefully measured. Whether this is discussion with others who share my faith in Jesus, what He is calling them to do, or who this person is who captured my heart and saved my soul, the backdrop of creation is a canvas to invite people to meet the Creator.

Mint Chocolate Brownies Serves 32

You will need a baking tray. I use a 40x27cm glass Pyrex roasting dish – the sides should be about 5cm high. Line this dish with greaseproof paper.

Ingredients

1 box mint Matchmakers

200g dark chocolate

50g milk chocolate

225g butter

325g golden caster sugar

4 eggs

175g plain flour, sifted

Method

1. Preheat the oven to 190C/170C fan/gas mark 5.

2. Chop the mint Matchmakers into small pieces, about 0.5cm in length. If some get crushed, don't worry, it all adds to the flavour.

3. Break the dark and milk chocolate into a heatproof bowl and place this above a bowl of gently simmering water until it melts. Also melt the butter at this point.

4. Place the sugar and eggs in a large mixing bowl and whisk until they are light and fluffy.

5. Add melted butter and melted chocolate to the sugar and egg mix. Using a hand whisk, combine the ingredients.

6. Add about half the flour and gently fold it in until the mixture is smooth. Add half the chopped Matchmakers and continue to fold. Then add the remaining flour and Matchmakers and fold until the mixture is fully integrated.

7. Bake on the middle shelf of the preheated oven for 40 minutes, or until a skewer comes out of the batch clean.

8. Leave to cool in the tray for 10 minutes before turning out onto a cooling rack. Once fully cool, slice into pieces (I suggest 32).

9. Enjoy!

Fusion food unites a marriage

'How good and pleasant it is when God's people live together in unity!'
(Psalm 133:1)

Caribbean food generally involves a lot of marinating and this is no exception, as it is normally prepared the day before to let it marinate overnight. The fact that I cook it in the slow cooker too means it teaches us all patience as we smell the flavours coming through the kitchen but have to wait patiently to actually eat it!

The dish originated in South East Asia and has become popular as one of the signature dishes of Caribbean food through the Indian diaspora. The cuisine of the Caribbean has been heavily influenced by South East Asian cuisine, with curries and roti prevalent throughout the islands and the use of similar high levels of spices for many dishes.

As I'm Caribbean and married to a Sri Lankan, this felt a natural dish to make at family parties for my new extended family after I got married, to help bring unity. The combination of South East Asian and Caribbean tastes represents our marriage itself and it always brings a smile to my husband's face.

Caribbean Curried Goat Serves 6 to 8

Ingredients

2kg goat meat on the bone

1 lemon

2 tablespoons cumin

4 tablespoons hot curry powder

1 tablespoon turmeric

1 tablespoon ground coriander

1 tablespoon ginger powder
or thumb-size of chopped
fresh ginger

1 cup red wine vinegar

1 cinnamon stick

Fresh thyme

1 large onion, chopped

6 cloves garlic, finely chopped

4 cloves

½ tablespoon fenugreek seeds

1½ tablespoons chilli powder

5 small potatoes, cubed

½ can coconut milk

2 scotch bonnets

2 bay leaves

2 bruised cardamom pods

1 lamb stock cube

Salt and pepper to taste

Handful coriander or parsley
to garnish

Method

1. Trim excess fat from goat.

2. Squeeze lemon and wash meat with water and lemon juice.

3. In a large bowl add the washed meat, cumin, curry powder, turmeric, coriander, ginger (fresh or powder), red wine vinegar, cinnamon stick and fresh thyme.

4. Stir well and cover bowl with cling film.

5. Allow to marinade in the fridge overnight.

6. Transfer the seasoned meat into a crockpot.

7. Add chopped onion, chopped garlic cloves, cloves, fenugreek seeds, chilli and cubed potatoes, and stir.

8. Set the slow cooker on for 8 hours.

9. After 3 hours cooking add the coconut milk, 2 whole scotch bonnets, bay leaves and bruised cardamom pods.

10. Cover and leave to cook.

11. Add lamb stock cube.

12. Taste and adjust the flavour, adding salt and pepper as required.

13. Serve in a bowl and garnish with fresh chopped coriander or parsley.

14. Serve with rice and peas or fresh rotis and a mint sambal.

Something I was created to do

For me, there's nothing better than inviting people round for a dinner party. The opportunity to cook, entertain and go deeper over food. Whether it's friends, family, acquaintances or strangers, there's something wonderfully special in connecting with people and sharing food around the dinner table.

It's so difficult in a large London church to build friendship and community. The church service is over and you are ushered out as the next service is about to start. The space isn't always there to get to know people. I spent four years attending a service where I knew people to say hello to on a Sunday; I was part of a hosting team and served in the café, but the connections were superficial – I didn't really know what was going on in their lives and I didn't share what was really going on in mine. It was not until I started connecting with people around the dinner table that I started to develop relationships and go deeper.

I love to invite a mix of people – close friends, people from the church that I don't know but would like to get to know better, believers, not-yet believers, neighbours, friends of friends, married people, single people. Some of my closest friends started out as strangers at one of my dinner parties, but the bonds created around the dinner table mean that they will be friends for life. The invitation from Psalm 34:8, 'Taste and see that the LORD is good', is something I offer all my guests. To taste of the fruit of the earth and the delicious roast lamb recipe and also to taste of shared hopes and dreams; of personal testimonies of faith and trust in the kingdom.

My go-to recipe for hosting dinner parties is always slow-roasted lamb with roast potatoes, greens and tangy mint sauce. Everyone has a memory of a good roast dinner, and for many people it harks back to childhood Sunday roasts. It evokes a sense of warmth, homeliness and family.

Over the years I have cooked for hundreds and have found it such a great way to connect with people and build relationships. Sitting around a dinner table over food creates a wonderful community environment. It becomes a place where bonds are formed, relationships grow and each person has the opportunity to be part of the family.

And for me, as I began to invite people for dinner I started to grow in the ability to throw a good dinner party. Every time I have people round for dinner, it makes me feel like I am doing something I was created to do. It makes me come alive! I have cooked many different recipes for dinner parties, but I always come back to the roast dinner. It's what people love, and everyone so enjoys eating it.

Slow-roasted Leg of Lamb Serves 8

Ingredients

Leg of lamb (1.8-2kg will serve 8)

12 cloves garlic

Handful fresh rosemary

600ml lamb or beef stock

Olive oil

Salt and pepper

Method

1. Preheat oven to 160C/140C fan/gas mark 3.

2. Place lamb in roasting pan.

3. Drizzle a very small amount of olive oil over the lamb and rub in to coat lightly.

4. Season both sides of the joint with salt and pepper.

5. Take a sharp knife and make about 8 2cm deep incisions around the joint.

6. Place a garlic clove in each incision.

7. Place half the rosemary and the remaining garlic cloves underneath the joint.

8. Place the lamb leg fat side down on top of the rosemary and garlic (this part has the most meat and will cook in the liquid).

9. Pour the stock into the bottom of the roasting dish and place the remaining rosemary on top of the meat.

10. Cover with 2 sheets of tinfoil to create a tight seal.

11. Place in the centre of the oven and slowly cook for 4-5 hours.

12. Check halfway through cooking time to make sure the pan is not drying out. If it is, add a small amount of water to the bottom of the pan.

13. Once cooked, the meat should fall off the bone easily with a spoon.

14. Use the juices left in the pan to make the gravy.

15. Serve with roast potatoes, green vegetables, gravy and mint sauce.

Crispy Roast Potatoes Serves 4

Ingredients

1.5kg floury potatoes (such as King Edward or Maris Piper)

200g goose fat or lard (or vegetable oil for vegetarians)

Salt

Method

1. Preheat oven to 220C/200C fan/gas mark 7.

2. Peel potatoes.

3. Leave potatoes fairly large. Cut any very large potatoes into roughly 6-8cm chunks.

4. Rinse in cold water.

5. Place in a large saucepan with just enough cold water to cover the potatoes. Add a pinch of salt.

6. Bring the water to the boil and when boiling, turn the heat down to simmer the potatoes for 2 minutes, or until the outer few millimetres of the potatoes are soft. You don't want to cook the potatoes – if you boil too long the potatoes will turn to mush and you will not be able to make roast potatoes out of them.

7. While waiting for the potatoes to boil, place the fat in a large roasting pan and put in the oven to heat up.

8. Once the potatoes are boiled, drain and put the drained potatoes back into the saucepan.

9. Shake the potatoes in the saucepan to roughen the edges. This creates a larger surface area for the fat to stick to, creating nice crispy roast potatoes.

10. Take the roasting tin out of the oven. Carefully tip the potatoes into the hot fat. Be very careful as the fat may spatter and scald.

11. Use a spoon to turn the potatoes in the fat, coating thoroughly, and ensure they are spread in a single layer with room between each potato. Lay so that the smallest edges are touching the bottom of the pan.

12. Roast in the hot oven for 45 minutes – 1 hour or until golden and crispy.

13. Remove from the oven, sprinkle with salt and serve.

'They ate to the full
and were well-nourished;
they revelled in your great goodness'

Nehemiah 9:25

I was in my home church at our weekly communion service. It was a solemn and sober occasion. Most of the men were wearing suits, the women wearing hats. There were long periods of silence punctuated by long prayers and hymns accompanied by an organ. As a ten-year-old kid, I was fairly bored. I had attended this service, and the other two Sunday services, every week since I was born, so I knew what to expect. At 10.50am we would pass the bread and the wine round, and all baptised adults would take a piece of bread and sip the surprisingly strong wine, in remembrance of Jesus. We were eating and drinking at the 'Lord's Table'. I would enjoy watching one of the old ladies have an unnecessarily big gulp of the wine, and see the crumbs left in the cup as my mum had her sip. I noticed some adults pass the elements on without taking part.

What was on my mind, however, was the bring-and-share lunch afterwards. My church was a Brethren church, and one thing the Brethren are renowned for is their buffets. In store for me in an hour's time was a smorgasbord of culinary delights provided by Salford's finest Christian cooks. I could already smell the sausage rolls and chicken legs cooking in the kitchen. There would be cheesecakes and trifles, more than enough for everyone. As we processed through to eat, the atmosphere lightened. The serious-faced men in suits loosened up and began to tell jokes and laugh together. The husband of one of the church members – he himself didn't come to church – arrived to share lunch with us. Some of the kids who had been giggling in the meeting sat with the old folks who had been scowling at them, but now they were all laughing and talking together.

As a young kid I distinctly remember looking around the room that day and thinking, 'I prefer this table in here to Jesus' table in there. It's much more fun, and everyone is welcome.' I felt a bit guilty at the time for thinking such an ungodly thought, but it has stayed with me to this day and profoundly affected the way my faith has developed, and the practice of the church that I now lead.

Fast-forward twenty years from that moment. You are at the first-ever gathering of Langworthy Community Church in Salford. Langworthy is a sprawling estate with rows upon rows of red-brick terraced houses, and is known around the area for extremely high levels of crime and deprivation. There is a team of fifteen people who are serving out shepherd's pie, and to our delight some guests from the estate have come along. One lady is drunk, and proceeds to heckle me throughout my talk. Another lady arrives, notices there are spare seats and calls her friends and five more turn up! A toddler runs round shouting the 'f' word very loudly! But we are all fed, and Jesus is with us. I assumed the chaos would settle down after a few weeks, but for the fourteen years since then, each Sunday has been pretty much a case of food, fun, noise and Jesus in the midst of it all.

As we started off on a journey of planting a church in an area where most people were desperate to leave, we were convinced that if we were going to reach this community (for whom God had broken our hearts), it would be

A table of hope

around a table. This is what Jesus did, and we are followers of Jesus. The table was the place where Jesus demonstrated, in word and deed, what the kingdom of God was all about. The table was the place where the outcasts and the ragamuffins came and found love, acceptance and transformation. Jesus' table was the place of healing and wholeness, where the most despised became the most honoured guests.

Jesus' table was a place of hope. In a world where you could measure your identity and position in society by who you ate meals with and where you sat in relation to the host, Jesus ate with sinners, tax collectors and prostitutes. He told His followers to seek the lowest place at banquets, the direct opposite of what they would have been taught by their parents. He ate with slaves and children, and probably with Gentiles too, breaking all the social taboos of His day and outraging the religious and political leaders. Have you ever outraged anyone by who you eat with? Jesus was criticised for eating with tax collectors and sinners, and accused of being a glutton and a drunkard because of the people He included in His community. Following Jesus involves us doing the same thing.

> When I give money to charity, or even a couple of hours a week volunteering, it eases my conscience and genuinely helps others. But it doesn't change my life

This is not easy. It is much easier to fill our tables (and our lives) with people who are similar to us. People we like, who hold similar opinions, who make us feel good. But Jesus is doing something different, something deeper, something which is ultimately going to mess up our lives if we follow Him in this. It's one thing to have our church outreach programmes – a foodbank, an annual Christmas meal for the homeless, a weekly street outreach. They are all so important. But Jesus is not just doing some charitable activities here. When I give money to charity, or even a couple of hours a week volunteering, it eases my conscience and genuinely helps others. But it doesn't change my life in the way Jesus is modelling. Jesus is modelling a way of life that isn't simply about doing good deeds for people, but actually opening our lives and homes to people who may be very different to us. This can be an uncomfortable place to be, but if we are willing to fill our tables with those who are 'other', there we will meet the risen Jesus. 'For I was hungry and you gave me something to eat, I was thirsty and you gave me something to drink, I was a stranger *and you invited me in*' (Matthew 25:35, my emphasis).

The earliest Church expected to meet the risen Jesus around the meal table, and in the face of strangers. Lots of Jesus' resurrection appearances involve food. Look at the road to Emmaus story in Luke 24. The two disciples offer hospitality to the stranger on the road, and Jesus is revealed to them in the breaking of bread, when they welcome the stranger and eat with Him. Hospitality is key to encountering Jesus, and healing is strongly linked to hospitality too. In fact, it would seem that healing and hospitality are like two sides of the same coin. When Jesus sends out the seventy-two, He commands them to go to a house, eat what is set before them, then heal the sick. Meals and miracles belong together in the ministry of Jesus. Transformation happens at His table. Look what happened to Zacchaeus when he had Jesus round for tea! It cost him a lot of money but he was utterly changed forever.

Over the years as we as a church have eaten together each Sunday, we have encountered the risen Jesus around the table. Whereas in Jesus' day the Pharisees sought to protect their holiness by excluding anyone unclean, Jesus did the opposite and deliberately invited the outcasts and the unclean to eat with Him. He reached out and touched them. And the wonderful thing here is that they didn't make Jesus unclean. He made them clean! In Jesus' kingdom and around His table, holiness becomes contagious!

This is a wonderful thing. Often Christians can be afraid of the world and worried they will be polluted and corrupted. The good news that Jesus brings is that in His kingdom, we need not be afraid of the world ever again! 'The one who is in [us] is greater than the one who is in the world' (1 John 4:4:). We can go to the darkest and most difficult places and bring the wonderful holiness of Jesus, bringing hope and healing and transformation. We can share our tables and our lives with people who are utterly different to us, and Jesus Christ will meet us there. Will we allow Jesus' example of hospitality to challenge and disturb our lives today, so that we might meet Him as we welcome the stranger and outcast to the table?

Families that eat together grow together

As a pastor's wife and mum to four lively children, the kitchen table was one of the most important places in our house for growing and nurturing our family. Almost every day of the week we set aside an hour to be together, to share stories about our day, what we had learned, seen, encountered, who we had spent time with, and how it had made us feel, while we ate a meal together.

It often began with moans and groans as I called them away from the TV, friends or homework to lay the table and wash their hands before sitting down together around our old pine table on an assortment of chairs. For at least half of the week we would have guests share a meal with us, either school friends or people who were staying in our home, so we learned lots about welcoming the stranger and opening not just our home but also our hearts and conversations to others who were able to introduce us to stories and ideas beyond our usual discussions.

Eating together as a family teaches us a number of values and qualities that help us as we negotiate adulthood. We learn to eat a variety of foods, to accommodate the tastes of others and not just our own, and so gain understanding that we can't always have the things we want. We learn that there are a multitude of ways to prepare food and live out our lives and that it is important to value diversity not just on the plate and around the table, but to extend these lessons into life beyond the kitchen walls. We learn the art of communication not just with our peers but also with other generations, thereby giving us confidence to share and contribute in many of life's varied opportunities. We listen and learn about facts and feelings as siblings, parents, friends and strangers tell stories about their lives, their day, the joys and the difficulties. We learn how to discuss, debate and negotiate life by hearing and observing how those we love have grown through situations that we might later come to face. We learn how to argue without walking away, and to value the opinions of others even when we disagree.

The kitchen table is a place for giving thanks, not just for the food we are about to eat but also for the lives of those whom we encounter, either in person or via the real-life stories we hear throughout the day. It is a place where after we have eaten, chatted, laughed and complained together, we can bring our thoughts before God and ask that He would bless us and care for us and grow us together in love.

It is also a place to learn responsibility and what it means to have a servant heart as we all partake in the washing of dishes, soap bubble fights and tea-towel leg flicks, accompanied by deep theological and philosophical questions about the meaning of life from the perspective of a ten-year-old, with answers provided by both a fourteen-year-old and a five-year-old that result in yet more questions. It is an opportunity to share your inmost thoughts about what God has shown you and how much He loves each of your precious offspring that He has trusted into your care.

So next time you sit around the table together, give thanks to God for your family, and remember that this is more than just a time to feed our bodies, but an occasion to nourish the soul and nurture and grow our children to become the people God has created them to be.

'This must be what family feels like'

Food has always been central to our church. In fact, Unlimited Church in Exeter has never held any form of church service or meeting without food of some kind being involved. And it is not particularly because we ourselves are that interested in food. We are just convinced it is a brilliant way of bringing people together, loving them and valuing them, and encouraging community.

In 2007 my husband James and I moved from Birmingham to Exeter with our two sons, Joshua and Toby, to start a church for young people who 'don't do church'. Our first attempts involved us walking around Exeter city centre approaching, often tentatively, groups of young people and asking them if they were willing to talk to us. We would ask them what they thought about church. What they would like to see in a church designed around young people. What they thought about God. What they thought He thought about them. And if it was appropriate, we would offer to pray for them. We would listen with our hearts open to hear what God might want to speak into their lives.

But we quickly realised that we could only get so far with this model. We needed a building to invite the young people into. A place that could be church – and family. Miraculously we were offered the rental of a small room attached to a city-centre church. We had a vision of a youth café. So we decorated, added pictures and scatter cushions, bought hot chocolate, cream and marshmallows.

To our great joy, almost from the first week of having this café God brought young people along. My memories are of that small room being filled with much laughter. We became skilled at making hot chocolate mountains, mugs overflowing with cream and marshmallows. And we just spent time with the young people. Shared our lives. Week after week young people returned, trusting us enough to invite their friends. We talked to them about our faith. We gave them a safe space in which it was good to ask questions. Everyone who came was offered prayer if they wanted it.

From the start we always tried to have home-baked cakes. All the team were involved in baking – students cooking in their halls of residence, the older members around other work commitments. None of us found it is easy. I became skilled at making large numbers of double chocolate chip muffins. I was perhaps even better at making Victoria sponge cake, but it was never as popular! We persisted in making the cakes ourselves, even when it would have been easier and perhaps cheaper to buy them from the local supermarket, because we wanted everything about that room, that space, to be the very best it could be.

Many of the young people we were meeting had broken and dysfunctional families. We were staggered at how difficult many of their lives were. We were heartbroken by their stories. And we were called to be family to them, to be a safe haven in their week, and I wanted the people who came to learn something of their value through the quality of what they received from us. I wanted them to know they meant more to me, to God, than some powdered coffee and a packet of biscuits. That even before they arrived I had invested time, thought, money and energy into them. In short, that they mattered.

In time, some of the youth who came to the café became Christians. One day, one of them, Jess, turned to a team member as we were sitting together and eating and said, 'I guess this must be what family feels like', and in that instant I knew that we had got it right. We were called to be Church, to be family to these young people, and Jesus had used home-baked cakes to make it happen!

Tim's Amazing Chocolate Brownies

Tim is a vital and vivacious member of Unlimited Church and these are one of our favourites! We know they are unhealthy but occasionally that is OK! We all prefer them on the gooey side of cooked. For these fantastic creations to achieve perfection, Tim's trick is to use a deep pan so that the brownie is too thick to ever set properly.

This recipe is designed to feed a crowd. It can easily be easily halved.

Ingredients

500g soft unsalted butter

500g best quality dark chocolate

8 large eggs

1½ tablespoons vanilla extract

660g caster sugar

300g plain flour

1½ teaspoons salt

400g chopped walnuts

Method

1. Preheat the oven to 180C/160C fan/gas mark 4. Grease and line a roasting tin or traybake tin. These quantities will more than fill a 30x25cm deep pan.

2. Place the butter and chocolate into a large heavy-based saucepan, and gently melt.

3. In a bowl, beat the eggs with the vanilla and sugar.

4. Into another bowl, measure the flour, and add the salt.

5. When the chocolate mixture has melted, remove it from the heat and let it cool slightly. Then beat in the egg and sugar mixture.

6. Add the nuts and flour and beat well to combine all the ingredients. Transfer to the lined tin.

7. Bake for about 25 minutes. When the top has dried to a paler brown but the middle is still gooey, the brownies are ready. Be careful not to overcook the brownies as they will continue cooking in the tin even after you have removed them from the oven.

8. Let them cool in the tin, and then mark into squares and enjoy. Delicious while still warm!

Sharing
living bread

YEMI ADEDEJI

Cook for love and eat in love

'm reminded of how my mother's expression of her love for me has always been through her detailed effort to cook a variety of food whenever I'm visiting her. Even as a ninety-one-year-old, her first statement to me when she knows I will be visiting her is, 'Be ready to eat a specially prepared meal on your arrival.' Her expression of love is in cooking for me, and my expression of love to her is in eating her specially prepared food until I can eat no more.

Whenever I'm abroad and about to return home, my wife will ask the same question she always has: 'What would you want to eat on your return?' Her love for me will make her go the extra mile to prepare whatever I may have requested, and you can see the joy on her face as I clear my plate and ask for more.

I seldom cook for my family but do so at weekends if I'm at home. How much I love surprising them with my specially formulated breakfast menu! I can recollect numerous conversations and cries of, 'I love you, Dad!', from my daughters whenever the opportunity has arisen.

The power of cooking for love and eating for love can never be underestimated. Food is a means of building relationships and exploring deeper fellowship that may lead to a long-lasting relationship.

My first date with my wife before we got married twenty-nine years ago was an invitation to her for dinner that I cooked specifically to impress her, and also to demonstrate my love and affection. She barely touched the food, but the relationship that we have today started from her acceptance to join me at the table and eat with me. I'm not sure how brilliant my cooking was, but I remember spending the whole day preparing beans and dodo (fried plantain) with grilled chicken with a taste of African pepper in tomato sauce.

The outcome of my expression of love that was demonstrated in my cooking and eating with her was a journey that we started which has now produced three wonderful girls and a loving home.

In the Scriptures, it's interesting that Jesus' ministry paid attention to sitting together and eating. Whether in the turning of five loaves of bread and two fish into a meal that fed thousands of people, or in eating together with the disciples in the upper room at the Last Supper to initiate a continuous communion with Him whenever we break bread and drink wine, or in Jesus becoming a chef who prepares a meal and welcomes His disciples after resurrection, Jesus at various times demonstrated the power of fellowship, love and companionship through food and when eating together.

It is instructive in my culture back home in Africa that you never eat without offering

people around you the opportunity to share your meal. 'E wa bawa jeun' in the Yoruba language from western Nigeria is a common phrase around food. It simply means, 'Come and join me to eat.' If, while eating, a visitor arrives, it is considered inappropriate to continue to eat without inviting the visitor to join in.

Some food is special to particular seasons, events, ceremonies or based on the importance of a visitor. One's love for a particular relationship or visit will often determine the type of preparation employed in preparing such food.

The varieties of such food prepared will often range in delicacies. Many things emerge while having fellowship around food, especially when an opportunity arises to cook and eat with a friend who is yet to become a follower of Jesus.

I remember a while ago when I visited a friend who was then not a Christian. She prepared a sumptuous meal for me. I asked her, while still cooking, why the effort to sacrifice her time and money to prepare and cook for me? Her reply was simply because of her love for me. I then informed her of another food, spiritual food prepared thousands of years ago for everyone by God through Christ Jesus. She asked me to share further, and I took the opportunity of her cooking to draw parallels, explaining the love in salvation as food prepared by Jesus when He died on the cross for anyone who would like to eat. She kept on probing over the meal, and by the end of the visit she asked whether she could eat the food prepared by God through Christ's death and resurrection. She believed in her heart and confessed Jesus as Lord with a renewed love that transformed her life the same day.

I've always thought about the unending opportunity of sharing Jesus over a simple meal with friends, family, neighbours and loved ones who are not Christians. A guided conversation around love towards friends when we invite them to dine with us because of our love for God may end up seeing many of our guests seek the Saviour, and probably many more will become followers of Jesus.

Food prepared in love will welcome people to eat in love, and a fellowship of love can deepen our love for Christ. It will also expose others to the love that God gave through Christ Jesus.

Text-a-toastie: divine deliveries

Picture the scene: you're in halls, powering through the final chapter for tomorrow's lecture, and someone offers you a hot, oozy, melted cheese toastie, delivered straight to your door. Sounds pretty good, right?

Meet 'text-a-toastie'. It's an ingenious initiative run by Christian Unions (CU) across the country in universities, colleges and schools, and the idea is pretty simple: for a whole evening, if you text a question about Christianity with your address and choice of toastie filling, a member of the CU will deliver your toastie along with a response to your question … all for free!

Whether it's somebody asking a silly question for a free toastie, a debate-aholic who wants a good argument, or someone genuinely curious about Jesus, the CUs try their hardest to deliver to everyone. From personal experience, I can say that text-a-toastie events regularly catalyse great conversations about faith in Jesus. I didn't get to share the gospel in full every time, but I did sometimes, and that's worth celebrating!

So why does text-a-toastie work? Why do people consistently engage with faith through it? Why hasn't it got old and stopped working?

Well, it's mainly because the gospel is compelling and life-changing, and God blesses the boldness of the Church when we go and share it. But I tell you what else makes text-a-toastie work: the free toasties!

Because, you see, without the food, nobody would text in their questions about faith – except the aforementioned hardcore debate-aholics, that is! The hospitality of free food opens up conversations with those who might not chat with us otherwise. Sharing food with someone on their corridor, or in their room with friends, creates a space where we can then share our thoughts on life and faith, asking questions and offering responses.

Ultimately, I think speaking to someone about the gift of grace is so much easier after offering them a free gift of food; the blessing of food is symbolic of the blessing of the love of Jesus. Like Mephibosheth at David's table, we have been invited to the Lord's Table, in His presence. The meal is a symbol of what it is like to be with God and 'taste and see' His goodness. What better basis to share Jesus?

Free food touches the heart of everyone, not just the cheapskate student. The CU at my university offered free food at almost all of its events, so much so that people genuinely started to believe it was a scam and there must be catch! But what a testament to God's people that we are so radically generous, so abundantly lavish in our hospitality, that people think it's too good to be true!

It might not be text-a-toastie, dial-a-donut, call-a-crêpe, buzz-a-brownie or message-a-mince pie to fuel last-minute essay-writing, but how could we demonstrate the generosity of God through hospitality wherever we are? How could we create space for fruitful conversations, and the chance to share Jesus as we share food?

'Jesus said to them,
"Come and have breakfast."'

John 21:12

Meals constrained by love

I t only dawned on me recently that there is actually a link between eating and drinking communally, and human health and well-being. Apparently, eating together taps into something deep in our shared humanity. It's a primal instinct which almost carries a sort of 'spiritual' component that isn't easy to define. It's something that is 'better felt than telt', as a Scot would put it. My best shot at this is to say that a profound sense of communion takes place when people eat together. It may be more of a convenient social function in Western societies, but it's embedded deeply as a cultural norm in peoples with family roots in other parts of the world.

The Bible helps us understand the importance of eating because it has so much to say about food and drink. Food was instrumental in the great rebellion in the Garden of Eden – the remedy to which is celebrated at the 'wedding supper of the Lamb' (Revelation 19:6-9). God fed the ancient Jews in the wilderness with manna – the food of angels (Exodus 16:31). Food and water were brought by an angel to Elijah as part of his recovery from exhaustion and depression (1 Kings 19:5-7). Food was and is part of the fabric of Israeli religious life – for example, the Seder meal at Passover and the weekly Shabbat family meal. And it is found in other faith traditions as well. For Muslims, the breaking of the daily fast during Ramadan, together with the feast at the end (Eid al-Fitr), puts food at the centre of spiritual life, and the Hindu celebration of Diwali would not be complete without food. Even for the non-religious, food is used to mark social occasions such as birthdays, anniversaries, retirements, wedding receptions, christenings or wakes.

There is an old adage, 'As in the natural so in the spiritual', and this holds good in that food sustains our physical frame biologically, just as spiritual food sustains and nourishes our soul. In this way it seems true to say that food and faith belong together.

It's in this context that we can understand Jesus' announcement, 'I am the bread of life' (John 6:35). He brought natural and spiritual food together – in Himself. Eating with His friends seemed to characterise His life, to the point that His critics accused Him of being a 'glutton and a [boozer]' (Matthew 11:19). At a wedding reception in Cana, He was responsible for providing such quality drink that people said that the best wine had been kept to last (John 2:10).

Jesus performed a miracle of provision of multiplied bread for a crowd of more than 5,000 Jews and, on another occasion, one for more than 4,000 people, many of whom would have been Gentiles. When Jesus raised a girl from the dead, He instructed people to 'give her something to eat' (Luke 8:55). After raising Lazarus, He stayed for dinner with his family (John 12:2). His whole life seemed to be punctuated by meals with friends, and sometimes even those from a different cultural heritage. At the end of His earthly life in His incarnate physical body, Jesus celebrated the Passover with friends in an upper room. It was a party we now call the 'Last Supper'.

Jesus modelled a lifestyle in which food united the Great Command to 'Love your neighbour' (Matthew 22:39) with the Great Commission to reach your neighbour (Matthew 28:19) as He simply ate with people. We usually eat with people we love, or like, or at least know well enough. In this environment something special can take place, which may be part of God's design for us as human beings since the creation. It's in eating together that our spiritual as well as our physical needs are in some sense ministered to. If we believe Him, we are instructed to 'live as Jesus did' (1 John 2:6) and He called people His friends (John 15:15).

Eating a meal with a friend is the most natural thing in the world. The meal table can become a place in which authentic witness to Christ happens. I am not assuming only verbal witness here, but, more importantly, holistic witness. This is a whole-life approach, involving attitude, action and words that are used in that context – often by simply responding to questions from a friend (1 Peter 3:15).

> His whole life seemed to be punctuated by meals with friends, and sometimes even those from a different cultural heritage

This is what I call 'relational witness', where the good news about Jesus comes wrapped in a person who loves God. This is a Christly form of witness because it's earthed in a context of a trusting relationship. As this happens it would be uncomfortable to say, 'I'm your friend so that you will follow Jesus' – a popular understanding of so-called 'friendship evangelism'. Instead, we are able to say, 'I want you to follow Jesus because you're my friend, but even if you don't follow Jesus, I'll still be your friend.' The first attitude carries with it a warning that we are moving away from a form of witnessing that has integrity. The other attitude comes from a Christly disposition, which has both 'grace and truth' (John 1:14).

Relational witness in the setting of a meal is less forced. Neither is it born out of a sense of duty but rather out of a loving constraint (2 Corinthians 5:14). Here, witness to Christ starts way before we open our mouths to talk. Whole-life witness is a fusion of both actions and words. It is also less forced because we recognise we are not in the driving seat – the Holy Spirit is.

With all this in mind, relating the good news over a meal is not just pragmatic in the strategic sense but courteous in the human sense and Christly in the biblical sense.

EVE BALSHAW

For the love of the Lamb

Very shortly after becoming a vegetarian, I discovered two things:

1. I am now every host's least favourite dinner guest.

2. I am now every dinner guest's favourite topic of conversation: 'So why did you decide to give up meat?!'

Beyond the millennial trend of arbitrarily cutting out food groups, there are many reasons why people go vegetarian these days. Personally, however, if I was going to give up my beloved steak, then I needed more incentive than the latest fad diet!

As I settled into a life of tax-paying, contents insurance and other adult responsibilities, I quickly realised that my consumer choices matter. Sadly, however, we are rarely informed about the impact of eating meat, beyond its effect on our bodily health. Not only does the meat industry create more greenhouse gases than the transport industry, but the impact of a kilogram or two of British-bred beef is roughly the same as a flight from London to New York.

God has made us stewards of His creation, and while the environmental impact of excessive meat consumption is clear, we often forget that the people impacted by climate change are God's beautiful creations too. Climate change will devastate the lives of people living on low-lying land flooded by rising sea levels, and drastically affect farmers around the world whose lives depend on a good harvest – especially those without the finances to diversify in agricultural techniques.

Where you spend your money counts. It is a vote for the kind of world you want to live in, and I decided that I didn't want to fund a world where my hunger for a good burger came above my desire to love my global neighbours – even those I cannot see.

Jesus' death on the cross reveals God's love for us: a love that stopped at nothing to show us how valued we are. Becoming a vegetarian doesn't come anywhere close to the sacrifice Jesus made, but by my daily sacrifices I hope to better love God's valuable creations who are affected by my consumer choices.

I know forgoing meat isn't always the convenient choice, or even the juiciest, tastiest and most tender one, but it is the loving choice. Challenging yourself to give up meat for one day a week – or even just one meal a day – does make a difference. Not only that, but friends, family and colleagues will notice you've swapped ham for halloumi, or chicken for chickpeas, and ask you why.

And so, when I am inevitably asked, 'So why did you decide to give up meat?!', I get to share why I love God more than my own appetite. Why my partnership with Him in caring for creation is more important than my love of lamb shank. And why Jesus chose death on the cross to show His love for all humanity, inspiring me to reflect something of that same love when I choose what to put on my plate.

Everyone's Welcome Sweet Potatoes

The beauty of this hearty meal is that it works in any season, and it's so easy, you can focus on the conversation, not the cooking. It works for vegetarians (for vegans and lactose intolerants, just leave out the ricotta), as well as anyone at your table who has an allergy or chooses to abstain from some meat for religious reasons – so everyone's welcome!

When buying your groceries, try to avoid extra packaging and plastic; many of these ingredients can be bought loose or local. There are also no quantities for the ingredients, so it's easy to adjust to the number of people you're sharing your meal with.

Ingredients

Sweet potatoes (2 per person, preferably)

Coconut oil

Salt

Red onions

Mixed herbs

Baby tomatoes

Radishes

Bell peppers

Salad leaves (rocket, spinach and watercress are my favourite)

Olives

Ricotta

Method

1. Set the oven to 200C/180C fan/gas mark 6.

2. Wash the sweet potatoes, prick them with a fork several times, then cover them in coconut oil and sprinkle with salt. Place them in a roasting tray, and when the oven is up to temperature, put them in to cook for an hour.

3. As the sweet potatoes start to get all soft and oozy, chop up the onions and pop them in a pan on low heat with a couple of teaspoons of coconut oil. Season with salt and mixed herbs.

4. Wash the tomatoes and, once the onions are soft, throw the tomatoes in with them. When they start to cook, they'll soften so you can squash them with a wooden spoon to create a juicy sauce.

5. For the salad, simply quarter the radishes, dice the peppers and toss them in with the leaves. The pepperiness of the radishes and rocket works really nicely with the sweetness of the potatoes and the sharp creaminess of the sauce.

6. When the sweet potatoes are just about ready, throw the olives into the sauce, as many or as few as you like – they seem to split the crowd, but I love them! At the last moment before you serve, stir in the ricotta.

7. All that's left is to check that the potatoes are crispy on the outside and soft in the middle, then take them out and open them up. To plate, simply heap the sauce on top, and allow everyone to pile on some salad before they dig in!

With so many natural, unprocessed ingredients, this recipe is cheap, easy and allows for guilt-free seconds! You can experiment with the sauce by keeping the onion and tomato base, but adding ingredients such as mushrooms, chickpeas or extra cheese, or a favourite sauce. To feed more friends, just chuck more potatoes in the oven!

This recipe is so easy, really anyone could do it, but I like to think it still guarantees empty plates at the end … just promise me you'll follow it up with a cracking dessert!

A stepping stone to discipleship

I n September 2016, a men's small group from Kensington Temple church in Notting Hill organised a Curry Challenge in Bayswater. It's an annual event that presents the opportunity for members to invite unbelieving friends to be treated to an Indian curry, listen to a short talk, and hear a testimony, all while getting to know one another in an informal setting.

A few weeks before the event, one of my colleagues, while on our work break, was crying. When I asked if she was OK, she replied, 'I am worried about my son, Edwin, who is being badly bullied.'

Following an altercation and further continued bullying, Edwin had plummeted into deep depression and had been hospitalised on two separate occasions – one for two weeks and the other for three. The depression had deepened to the point where he wanted to take his own life.

Before our break ended, I told her that I was going to pray for Edwin. I also told her to tell her son that a colleague of hers was praying for him and wanted to meet with him when he was ready.

After a while I asked her how Edwin was doing. She said he was getting better so I asked if I could invite him to the curry night our group were holding. Edwin accepted the invitation.

On the day of the event, I picked Edwin up from his house and took him to the restaurant where the Curry Challenge was to take place. After a good meal, entertainment and fellowship, our leader shared his testimony, and Billy Graham (on a large screen in the restaurant) gave a short message on 'Hope'.

After this, I presented the guests on my table with an opportunity to give their lives to Jesus. Edwin gave his life there and then!

Every guest at the Curry Challenge evangelistic initiative was presented with a 'Welcome Bag'. We are very grateful to the Gideons who distributed some New Testament Bibles in these bags for our guests. Not everyone that night was as bold and evident as Edwin with giving their life to Christ, but I'm confident seeds of the gospel were sown in men's hearts. Being able to present these Welcome Bags containing the Bible provides an opportunity for them to delve into the Bible in their own time, thereby providing a pivotal link to give their life to Christ further down the line.

Another man on the night, having gone home with his Welcome Bag, placed the bag and Bible in a cupboard and forgot about them. Some weeks later, when he was home and alone with his thoughts, the curry night came to his mind. Intrigued, he pulled the bag out of his cupboard to look into its contents. He rang his friend who had invited him to the curry night, and said, 'I want to know more about this Jesus.'

Last week I saw him at Kensington Temple attending his first church service. The seeds had borne their fruit!

Edwin has not looked back and attends one of my men's groups each week as well as church every Sunday. He's a changed man and growing in Christ. Last month he was baptised.

We will keep praying that the Word of God will come alive in the lives of the other gentlemen to become fellow disciples in due season. Who knows when they will pick up that Bible – but we trust that one day they will, and will come to experience the great treasure of it, just as we have.

'Then God said, "I give you every seed-bearing plant on the face of the whole earth and every tree that has fruit with seed in it. They will be yours for food."'

Genesis 1:29

As someone who has always enjoyed a good meal with friends and family, the idea of a feast was an obvious inspiration when we were thinking of what to call our charity. The Feast is a Christian charity committed to helping teenagers from different religious backgrounds make friends, talk about faith and be peacemakers, changing the world around them. Eating is a big part of our events, which might be pizza whilst watching a film, a barbecue by the canal or a shared meal at an iftar as we end the fast during Ramadan with our Muslim friends.

Feasts of friendship and faith

The Feast 'Guidelines for Dialogue'

I will:

- *listen to what everyone has to say*

- *be honest in what I say*

- *speak positively of my own faith and beliefs, rather than negatively about other people's*

- *respect other people, even if I disagree with their views*

- *not treat people here as a spokesperson for their faith or culture*

- *not tell others what they believe, but let them tell me*

- *acknowledge similarities and differences between our faiths and beliefs*

- *not judge people here by what some people of their faith or community do*

- *not force everyone to agree with my views*

- *make every effort to get along with everyone regardless of their faith, gender, ethnicity or age*

Apart from having fun and eating, we help the young people learn how to talk about their faith openly and honestly to someone of a different religion. This also means being willing to listen to what the other person says and, in doing this, finding the similarities and differences in what we think and believe. In 1 Peter 3:15, we read that we should always be prepared to give a reason for the hope we have within us and that we should do this with gentleness and respect. This attitude of being ready to speak but being respectful and gentle is at the heart of how we help the young people share their faith.

Many people (of all ages) feel anxious about sharing their faith, concerned that they don't know enough or will cause offence. At The Feast, our way of working is to help the young people articulate their beliefs and understanding as far as they know them. We equip them to share their own faith rather than to try to copy a talk they heard or a clever argument they read about. All this is done in the context of making genuine friends, and there is no better way of doing that than when sharing food. One of the first questions we get the young people to answer is, 'What is the best thing about your faith?' This sets a positive

tone for the discussions and helps them share their thoughts and perspectives. We are very clear that there are no right or wrong answers, that it's simply about helping them share their beliefs. This respects the fact that everybody is at a different stage in their faith journey and that we all come from different cultures or faith traditions, and we want to help them share their faith authentically using language that they are comfortable with.

At every event we use our 'Guidelines for Dialogue' to set a framework for the discussions. This isn't done to limit or censor their comments, but to provide a safe space where they can share their faith honestly and with integrity.

We also include the following instruction: 'I understand that at any stage I can ask for a discussion to be stopped if I feel uncomfortable.'

In Matthew 9:10–11, we read that Jesus sat and ate with tax collectors and sinners, people the religious leaders thought were undesirable. We don't know what Jesus said to those He was eating with, but we do know that they chose to come to eat with Him. People of different faiths are not to be thought of as undesirable or 'sinners' – they are no more sinners than the rest of us. The challenge of verse 10 is to consider whether we would be willing to sit and eat with those that other religious leaders think we should avoid today. Sadly, I do hear church leaders warning against being too friendly with people of different faiths, or advising we only meet with them if it's specifically for evangelism. Yet here was Jesus just sitting and eating! But He clearly didn't hide who He was. As He said in response to the Pharisees in verse 12, He came not for the well but for the sick; His compassion was for those He was eating with, but it was expressed over the mutual sharing of a meal. Many of my Muslim friends would love me to convert to Islam and they know that I would love for them to follow Jesus as their saviour. But we share these ideas and beliefs through our friendship, over food and while being committed to a loving, genuine relationship that is not dependent on conversion.

This is the attitude we want to foster in the young people who come to The Feast – for them to be able to sit and eat together in a mutual, honest sharing that recognises the depth and passion of the faith we have. It's risky, fun, chaotic and unpredictable – in many ways like a very good feast.

Food has always played an important role in my life. Throughout my career of more than forty years in hospitality, I found any excuse to do something with food, whether that was at work or socially. It was really no wonder, therefore, that God used my love of food to draw me to a love for Jesus ...

It was twenty-five years ago that my husband and I first met, when he came into my restaurant for a coffee. After many years of forging careers, raising a family and perhaps being in a spiritual wilderness, my husband Neil and I decided it was time to reconnect with God.

As a result, I was guided to Christ Church, Felixstowe, and our first visit coincided with a shared barbecue to celebrate Father's Day. I'd been more focused on finding a church with wheelchair accessibility for Neil than anything else, but after the service, the minister invited us to stay for lunch, and God knew that that was exactly what we needed – we've never left!

It can be a daunting experience to go to a new church, especially if it's for the first time. Will I know what to say to people who seem to know more about God than I do? Is church really serious, or is it OK to laugh and have fun? That's why experiencing church for the first time through a shared lunch can be a wonderful, joyous way to meet Jesus in a relaxing, non-threatening environment.

We came home that first Sunday with full tummies, fuller hearts, and the knowledge of love and support from people who have now become great friends.

Food is a core theme throughout the Bible, from feasts and celebrations in the Old Testament to miracles that Jesus performed in the New Testament. While breaking bread and sharing food with His disciples and followers, Jesus told stories as only the master storyteller could, sharing the good news of God's provision and the great banquet that awaits all who follow Him (Luke 14).

So, Jesus was a feeder like me – not only of faith, but also of food! Just as we physically need food – a gift from God – to grow, nurture and survive, so we also daily need the feeder Himself, Jesus.

I have learned that food and faith are the perfect combination; it was food that first drew us into church, but it was God who kept us there. I am now a member of our hospitality team, and it's a joy for me to work with food, knowing that I'm helping to create the same welcoming environment for others that Neil and I first met Jesus through!

LUCY AGNEW

A gateway to God

NAOMI OSINNOWO

When I was ready to talk

'Will you tell me about Jesus?', or words to that effect, was what I asked a friend when I was ready to find out more. In the seven years leading up to that point, I knew there was a God, but I didn't know, or believe, that Jesus was the way – the only way – to Him.

This Christian friend of mine, whom I had known for five years by then, explained the gospel to me – not lectured, explained. Devoting at least three hours of his time during an evening telephone conversation, he took me on a journey that answered all my questions and covered, in immense detail, how I became separated from God, and my only way back to Him: by believing with my heart and confessing with my mouth that Jesus Christ is the Son of God.

It's not that I hadn't been told about Jesus before that evening in 2013. In fact, at least one person had shared a 'you have to believe or else' rendition of the good news with me. I had also tagged along with friends to church. But what I heard during those interactions or visits didn't hit home. What I needed (I now know) was a friend who was generous with their time, to take me on the 'lost to found' journey; a friend I trusted and whom I could ask questions. And that's exactly who God gave me.

I met 'J' in a community library in 2008, when I was almost twenty-three years old. I was feeling chatty, so despite the 'no talking' rule, I said hello. We ended up leaving the library together and taking a walk to a nearby Nigerian takeaway, as he was headed there to buy his evening meal.

Despite not being a big meat eater (I'm now a vegetarian), I ordered what he got: rice, an anonymous stew and plantain. We then went our separate ways. Admittedly, when I got the takeaway home, I managed to eat the plantain and a small amount of the rice, and left the rest.

I didn't know that would be the first of scores of meals J and I would share over the next five years, and up until now. We would meet after work, or in the afternoon on a Saturday, and walk, talk and head to a restaurant or café, where we would talk some more. We did the London restaurant circuit. We frequented Fortnum & Mason (his favourite for a while), The Wolseley (when Fortnum & Mason was closed), patisseries, burger joints, chains and independents. We ate Italian, Thai, Indian, Chinese (only once, as neither of us were keen), Turkish, European and Mexican. We even became regulars at some of these places.

The food wasn't always great, and there were times when it was plain awful. But dining out allowed us to hang out in a neutral setting, whatever the weather, and chat. Over a starter, I would explain to J what Teeline Shorthand is. Over a main meal, he'd share with me his fascination with domain names (I know). Over a dessert, or tea, we'd talk politics, local, national and global.

Doing this over and over again built up trust – a friendship – which meant that when I was ready to talk about Jesus, I could call J.

Lentils with Plantain (vegetarian and vegan) Serves 2

Ingredients

One cup red split lentils

1 onion

1 red and ½ green bell peppers

Garlic (bulb)

1 scotch bonnet/ fresh chilli or chilli powder

2 or 3 cardamom pods

Fresh lemon juice

Turmeric

Sea/pink salt

Rapeseed oil

Plantain (1 per person)

Method

1. Wash red split lentils in hot water until water is clear. Then run under cold water to get rid of all the hot water.

2. Submerge lentils in cold water (in a pan), with around 1½ inches above the lentils.

3. Bring lentils to the boil and allow to boil for some minutes. Reduce heat. Add salt, and allow lentils to slowly cook in the pot.

4. Remove from hob once the lentils are around 90 per cent cooked. There should still be water in the pot. If not, add.

5. While lentils are cooking, gently heat rapeseed oil in a pan. Once the oil is relatively hot, add diced/crushed vegetables in this order, stirring regularly: onion, bell peppers and garlic.

6. Fry on medium heat until vegetables are softened and slightly golden.

7. Empty lentils into pan with vegetables, and mix ingredients. The water from the lentils will have created a stock. If not, add a little. Add some flavour: scotch bonnet/fresh chilli (without the seeds) or chilli powder to taste, cardamom pods (2 or 3), a splash of fresh lemon juice, turmeric and salt. Stir and allow to simmer on a low heat.

8. While the lentil mix is simmering away, fry the plantain. Gently heat rapeseed oil in a non-stick frying pan. Remove skin from the plantain. Slice the plantain, diagonally, ¼ inch thick, and place into the heated oil to fry, on both sides. Plantain should be a dark golden brown.

The best evangelism we can do

The smell of freshly prepared Indian food was overwhelming our senses. We were soon seated around the table, tucking into what I still call 'the best food in the world'. There was laughter, smiles and lots of 'oohs' and 'aahs' as we loaded our plates and satisfied our appetites. Mum had made my favourite Indian dishes: lamb keema, yellow lentil curry, Bombay potatoes, coriander rice and fresh hot roti. The eight of us had just returned from a week of mission and, being teenage boys, we wanted nothing more than lots of good food. Gathering around the table, where my mum would always have food waiting, became a highlight of our return. These mealtimes became an opportunity for us to celebrate God's goodness as we would recount stories and testimonies of the mission trips we had just been on.

God could have made us like the plants so that we just absorbed nutrients through our feet – our 'roots' – but He is so good that He gave us the gift of eating – the pleasure of tasting, savouring and smelling our food. And this gift has been used throughout God's dealings with His people, in the Old and New Testaments, as an integral way of celebrating His goodness and faithfulness, of building community among believers, and leading many to come to faith in Christ.

In the Old Testament, there were three major feasts every year when God's people would gather together to worship Him – the Feast of Unleavened Bread, the Feast of Weeks and the Feast of Tabernacles – and each involved a lot of eating! It didn't matter what social class or standing a person had, all would come together during these times to honour God and delight in the good things He had blessed them with. 'Be joyful at your festival – you, your sons and daughters, your male and female servants, and the Levites, the foreigners, the fatherless and the widows who live in your towns' (Deuteronomy 16:14). Eating and rejoicing went hand in hand – 'There, in the presence of the LORD your God, you and your families shall eat and shall rejoice'

(Deuteronomy 12:7). God's goodness was not just some abstract theological truth, but rather something they could taste, savour and smell together.

The New Testament Church also made eating together a priority. We read in Acts 2:46-47 that, 'Every day they continued to meet together in the temple courts. They broke bread in their homes and ate together with glad and sincere hearts, praising God and enjoying the favour of all the people. And the Lord added to their number daily those who were being saved'. God's gift of salvation in Christ fills us with joy and gladness, and one way He knows we can celebrate this is by enjoying food together. I don't believe it is a coincidence that 'daily' salvations followed these mealtimes of genuine fellowship.

Beyond just the food was the implicit message being conveyed. The disciples were demonstrating the reality of the gospel that leaves the four walls of the temple and enters the personal living space. It was this sense of authenticity that became irresistible to a culture that knew only rules and regulations. I think it is authenticity that people are still longing for today. Perhaps the best evangelism we can do is to demonstrate the reality of the gospel by allowing His joy and hope to infiltrate our homes, our relationships, our daily living and eating. What would it look like if, instead of handing out flyers to events where someone may hear the gospel preached from a pulpit, we invited them into our homes so they could see the gospel through our lives?

> What would it look like if instead of handing out flyers to events ... we invited them into our homes so they could see the gospel through our lives?

Not only are there advantages of eating together, but, as we read in the New Testament, there is a great danger in failing to do so. It is interesting that Paul's challenge to the early Church on their division and inequality is followed by the advice that 'when [they] gather to eat, [they] should all eat together' (1 Corinthians 11:33). Eating together unites hearts, breaks down walls of inequality, and helps avoid divisions – something pointed to in the command of Deuteronomy where the servant, stranger, fatherless and widow are all to be invited to the table. Perhaps there are people in your life and even in your church that you struggle to get on with. Why not invite them over for a meal? There is something about the humility and vulnerability of welcoming them into your home that disarms and helps strengthen relationships.

We have tried to replicate this in our church family. There is rarely a leadership meeting or small group where food is not shared. Often we will have food at celebration services, because we recognise the importance of eating in opening up conversations and creating a space to really do life together – just as it did in those early mission days when our hearts grew closer as we reflected on God's goodness over my mum's great curry.

Eating together is God's idea. It points to His goodness and creates a space to share what is on our hearts. Eating together helps strengthen the unity of relationships and is a way of sharing the gospel with non-believers. I want to encourage you to be intentional about your eating. Perhaps you may decide to set aside one night a week where you invite someone over, whether that be a colleague, neighbour or even a gym buddy. Think about ways to intentionally use lunch breaks at work to demonstrate the joy of the gospel. However we decide to do it, let us eat together, and let us bring God glory together through our delight in His goodness and the authenticity we can share.

Tasting and seeing

Divine fruit salad

I love making fruit salad for dessert. Sometimes I make it for my family when my dad comes home from work, or for our neighbour who often pops round for a snack. My Divine Fruit Salad is a great way for me to tell others what Jesus means to me.

Spirit-filled Ingredients

2 bananas of self-control

5 juicy strawberries of love

1 green apple of peace

7 cherries of gentleness

9 grapes of goodness

2 kiwis of kindness

3 pears of patience

1 jackfruit of joy

A drop of your favourite faithful juice

Lyrical Method

To make a Divine Fruit Salad, begin with a smile.

When our neighbour comes round, my smile is long as the Nile.

He pulls up a chair and enquires about our day.

I reply, 'It was good, but only because we prayed!'

....

As I bring out a bowl and begin to prepare my fruits,

I explain to my neighbour how the Bible is the truth.

I start to peel my bananas of self-control,

And tell my neighbour how God cleansed my soul.

....

I top, tail and wash my strawberries clean,

Telling how God grows us from as small as a bean.

I start to slice my apple of peace thin,

And explain how God brought us out from sin.

Then I collect my cherries of gentleness and grapes of good,

And feel bubbly for by my side God has stood.

I begin to peel and slice my kiwis of kindness,

And explain that only God can deliver us from our blindness.

Then I core and chop my patient pears,

And explain to my neighbour that God really cares.

....

Next, I chop my joyful jackfruit,

And tell him God is my firm root.

A drop of my favourite faithful juice I add,

And tell my neighbour how God makes me glad!

....

Finally, I mix up the fruits in the bowl,

Give my neighbour a serving, refreshing his soul!

He takes a bite and smiles in delight.

He tells me he tastes Jesus' light!

O what a glorious night!

Jesus in me has burned bright!

'...the LORD your God will bless you
in all your harvest and in all the work
of your hands, and your joy
will be complete'

Deuteronomy 16:15

HELEN THORNE

Meals of thankfulness

For Ruth, the world seemed like a very bleak place. She was off work owing to ill-health, struggling financially to make ends meet, feeling increasingly socially isolated and slipping slowly into a pit of despair. There were days when she wondered if anyone would even notice if she ceased to exist – it didn't seem like anyone truly cared. Oh, there were professionals involved in her life; they all asserted that there were reasons to persevere, but friends were all so busy. The occasional text was small consolation in the hours she sat alone.

One day, an unexpected invitation came from friends at church: 'Would you like to join us for Sunday lunch each week?' The friends were quick to point out that it wouldn't be a fancy, stand-on-ceremony kind of meal. The kids would be screaming, the dog would be begging and the house certainly wouldn't have had a special clean. But Ruth was assured that if she could cope with the piles of papers, she would receive a warm welcome into the family and as many roast potatoes as she could possibly hope to consume.

It was an invitation too good to decline: an ideal opportunity to have regular contact with people she loved and healthy food at a time when making meals was tough – but what she discovered around that messy table was more than she could have imagined or hoped for.

The family had a tradition – no one quite remembers when it began. Before eating, everyone took it in turns to say something for which they were thankful. The objects of their thankfulness ranged widely: from family and food through toys and precious pet snails to Christ and all the riches that being in His kingdom brings. Each and every Sunday, Ruth was helped to smile as her friends expressed their thankfulness for the good things in their lives, and she was challenged to look for the good in hers.

The tradition had a cumulative effect. Over the weeks, Ruth's perspective changed. The tough things of her life didn't disappear, the pain and the hardship persisted in many ways, but her struggles began to be reframed. Rather than seeing all the tough stuff as the sum total of her experience, she started to see the pain as one facet of her life. Alongside, there were many things for which to be thankful – many things to praise God for – and sure and certain reasons to trust Him each and every day.

In biblical terms, she learned to worship in the way that Psalm 121 sets out. In the midst of her tears, she '[lifted her] eyes to the hills' (NKJV), to the Lord, and focused afresh on the one who could help her in her hour of need. And she did so, not in a seminar or in a service, but in front of a steaming plate of Yorkshire puds.

Food in the Bible often encourages people to focus on the goodness of God. Right back in Genesis 1, God gave people a huge diversity of plants to eat – it was a sign of His provision for the people He had made – and an aspect of the perfection of the pre-Fall world.

Even after the Fall, when human sin entered the world, He kept sustaining His chosen ones. A famine may have hit the known world, but He was able to put Joseph in just the right place and just the right position to ensure that His promises to build a nation did not fail.

Some years later, when the Israelites left Egypt and faced forty years of wandering in the desert, God gave them manna and quail from His mighty hand. They didn't always appreciate it, of course, but here too God in effect says to His people, 'I'm looking after you – and I am not going to stop.'

When they reached the Promised Land, they didn't find a nation barren and dry but a land 'flowing with milk and honey' (Exodus 3:8). Yet again, the Lord blessed His people with food. But as well as general provision, within that land, food was sometimes the object of miraculous provision – who can fail to be surprised at the prophet Elijah being fed by ravens, or by the jar of oil that never ran dry, both in 1 Kings 17?

Little wonder then that Jesus encourages His followers not to worry about what they will eat or drink (Matthew 6:25-26). There are, of course, injustices in this broken world, but ruling over it all is a God who provides for His people, and each piece of food we see can remind us of this glorious truth.

This provision of God goes beyond what God does, though, and strikes at the very heart of who God is. Jesus described Himself as the 'bread of life' and the Holy Spirit as 'living water' in the Gospel of John. Why? Because the physical food that we see is just a glimpse of something better. Lunch, wonderful though that is, pales into insignificance when compared to the sustaining nature of being in relationship with Christ.

You see, a slice of bread may keep us going for a few hours – the Bread of Life keeps us for eternity. In Christ, we move from being spiritually dead to spiritually alive both now and forever. He sustains far more than our stomachs; He sustains our very souls. As we see physical food, our minds are meant to be drawn to the wonderful, generous provision of God in all its aspects.

But it's not just that food is supposed to remind us of God's provision and God's providing nature – God has ordained that food is part of the way we are called to celebrate Him, too.

For the Israelites, feasting was an important part of community life. Whether that was celebrating God's goodness in giving a harvest, revelling in the beauty of weddings, or remembering His great acts of kindness to His people over time – corporate eating was an integral part of their life. The pinnacle, of course, was the Passover – an elaborate meal, dripping with symbolism as God's children remembered how He had rescued them from slavery in the past.

> Is it any wonder, then, that tables can be places of exceptional gratitude? Indeed, they should be places of transformational thankfulness

And for Christians too there is a continued call to share lives with our brothers and sisters (including eating with them) and show hospitality to those with whom we have far less in common.

The Passover is a meal that continues, in a new form, when we share the Lord's Supper today. It is as we eat and drink the bread and wine that we remember and celebrate Jesus' work on the cross and the glorious saving grace that frees us from slavery to sin. And it is there we also remember that His work has built us into a family, called to honour Him.

All this is a small foretaste of eternal life. There we can look forward to the victory banquet of Psalm 23 in a place where no one will ever again hunger or thirst (Revelation 7:16).

Is it any wonder, then, that tables can be places of exceptional gratitude? Indeed, they should be places of transformational thankfulness. There is pain for each and every one of us but, as we eat, each bite we take is a reminder of a God who provides for our bodies and souls – and every meal an opportunity to celebrate His goodness and grace with those He has placed around us.

Hot flavours bring life

As a Brazilian-American living in England, my Hot Sauce is very special to me – and something I like to bless others with. England is not generally known for its great food (sorry, but it's true). So I love bringing flavour and colour to people with my sauce. In many ways it's a representation of me, combining a Brazilian love of life and nature with an American practicality. It reflects a mixture of cultures, life and places where I've lived.

The sauce is really natural, really good for you, really tasty – and slightly addictive! My English husband just can't get enough of the stuff. It's made with entirely fresh and raw ingredients. No sugar. No salt. No cooking! Just lots of freshly squeezed lemons or limes, bunches of beautiful green parsley, masses of raw peeled garlic, lots of onions, various fresh chillies and also some Brazilian pickled chillies. It's simple because I believe that God has provided us with nature to supply us with everything our bodies need. This blessing for health and beauty is a direct expression of His goodness to us.

To me, preparing, mixing and blending these ingredients is not only therapeutic, it's like creating a work of art. Lots of art goes up on walls to be admired, and we wear forms of art. In this case, we eat it, and it's so very good for us. More than this, I believe God is not just interested in feeding us, He's also very interested in flavour. That's what I love about my Hot Sauce. It adds flavour and brings food to life – any food. It's a great marinade for chicken, fish or steak, brings life to salad dressings, and is awesome in soups. It's even great to spread on sandwiches.

I see my sauce as a great way of blessing my friends, family, neighbours and others. This is so easy and enjoyable to do, and it helps to start a conversation ... which will always at some point include Jesus. Whenever I'm in New York, I have to bring Hot Sauce for my young Muslim friend Hanifa. This has helped strengthen our relationship to the point that she's happy to go to church with me and even calls me 'Mom'. At home in our little English village, the sauce has helped build a number of relationships of trust with my neighbours. Even the postman is hooked on it!

Brazilian-American Hot Sauce

Ingredients

The precise quantities of the ingredients are subject to the maker's taste, but I ordinarily use:

4 heads peeled garlic

10 chopped onions

5 spring onions

Big bunch fresh parsley

Bag various fresh hot chillies

Bottle pickled chillies

1 cup apple vinegar

Juice 10 lemons or limes

1ltr extra virgin olive oil

Method

1. Chop and blend fresh garlic, onions, spring onions, parsley.

2. Remove from blender, and blend together fresh hot chillies and pickled chillies with apple vinegar, lemon or lime juice and olive oil.

3. Blend it all together into a paste – adding more olive oil to get a thick consistency.

Done. No sugar. No salt. No additives. No preservatives. No cooking.

Lasts ages. Just shake before use.

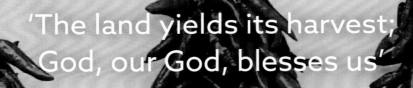

'The land yields its harvest;
God, our God, blesses us'

Psalm 67:6

Treating teens to the truth

My Sunday afternoon kitchen sets the scene – presenting a beautifully laid-out selection of delicious treats, ready and awaiting the arrival of six hungry and expectant teenage girls! Whether it's ice cream sundaes and squirty cream, pizza with toppings of their choice, or a chocolate fondue and retro sweets, they arrive knowing that it will be laid out with love and care for them as that wonderful gaggle of mid-teen girls take over my house for the afternoon.

While not haute cuisine, it'll be devoured and enjoyed amid the sharing of stories from the previous week – dissecting woes of exams and revision, or the tales of surviving teachers, friends and parents! While hardly pausing for breath, the treats are demolished as we chat before, as is our adopted tradition, adjourning to my lounge, where the sofas are ignored and the seven of us sprawl across the carpet, quite at home as we seek to further put the world to rights!

With happy and full stomachs – and a few hundred extra calories that will no doubt be worn off by the exercising of our mouths – we explore many a real-life issue around relationships, family, teen pressures and self-worth. All of this is against the backdrop of how we grow our character to be like Jesus, and put Him at the very centre of our lives. Prayer, mutual support and trust have been learned over the years within this safe space where, praise God, they feel they belong.

So why all the treats? Bad for their teeth?! Well, among many other things, twenty-plus years of youth ministry have taught me that when it comes to teenagers, you just don't scrimp on food. Foodie treats connect with the heart of pretty much any teenager – girl or boy. Whether out of a packet or lovingly prepared, the treats speak of love, of time together being important, and it instils value on the individuals who gather there. Food provides a centrepiece around which to sit and, even for those teens who might be unaccustomed to sitting at a table and eating together, food speaks of family, and valuing time together. It creates a safe space where a young person's opinions, life story and experiences can truly be heard.

To the savvy youth worker, food is a loving gesture and a great distraction. It detracts from the nervousness of a teenage girl who hasn't seen her friends for a while, or the one who arrives first and worries they're too early – these little things can create yet more anxiety in the world of a teen who's not as confident as she seems amid her circle of friends.

Over a smorgasbord of colourful cupcakes, pancakes or waffles, questions are posed, friendships are deepened, leadership is grown, mentoring flourishes, identity affirmed, individual gifting acknowledged, and Jesus is at the heart of it all. By His Spirit, Jesus is present, guiding our conversations and drawing us ever closer to Himself. As we share the fun of life and food together, and as love is lavished upon these girls in a tangible way, another scene is set, one for Jesus to graciously and abundantly unfold promise after promise to young and hopeful hearts.

'See what great love the Father has lavished on us, that we should be called children of God!'

(1 John 3:1)

Untroubled hosts and generous guests

When my husband and I first married, we would often have our most heated arguments about twenty minutes before we were due to have guests round. Having guests in my home was a new and stressful experience for me. I wanted everything to be just right, and didn't know how to cope if reality didn't live up to the picture in my head.

Martha too wanted to be a perfect host. She and her sister, Mary, were friends with Jesus; their brother was Lazarus, whom Jesus brought back from the dead, and they lived in a town called Bethany. In Luke chapter 10, we are told of the time Martha invited Jesus into their home. Martha was busy with the preparations, while her sister just sat with Jesus and listened to Him speak. She was so frustrated by the lack of support from Mary that she complained to Jesus that He should instruct Mary to help. But Jesus said no. Martha was 'worried and upset about many things' (Luke 10:41), but none of that really mattered. Few things are needed to host, and Mary had chosen right; to focus on Him, their guest.

There can be lots of reasons not to share a table with people. Maybe you worry that you're not a good enough cook or they won't like your food. Maybe you worry that your home isn't tidy enough, or impressive enough. Maybe you spend too much time fretting about how you will be able to make time to prepare for the meal, or how to afford it. Don't let distractions or excuses impinge on your opportunity to open yourself and your life to others.

In our house at the moment, the downstairs floor is cracked and broken, cabinet doors in the kitchen have fallen off. The windows all need replacing. The garden is more mud and weeds than lawn, and the kids seem forever intent on making my home look like a tornado just passed over. But when a load of school families came over for an impromptu barbecue, none of that mattered. Instead, our home was full of laughing kids and relaxing parents. People who had never spoken to each other before realised just how much they had in common, despite the fact that less than 20 per cent of the guests were even from the UK. One mum had been recently and very unexpectedly widowed. Chatting with us over food as her kids played in the garden, she confessed this was the first time she could begin to imagine a life that would be OK even without her husband. Jesus was in that place. None of the things I had worried about beforehand mattered in the slightest. It was an honour to host them and they were blessed by it.

Many of the most profound conversations I have had with people have happened around a meal table. Because, at the table, it becomes natural to offer your perspective based on your faith or your experiences of Jesus as part of the conversation. It becomes permissible to offer to pray into the situations recounted at the table. It becomes normal to speak of Jesus to others, because your life is shared at the table, and Jesus is the central part of your life. People can be themselves with friends, and strong friendships can be formed sharing food. The ebb and flow of conversation, as you share food together, allows poignancy and humour, history and personality to emerge with relatively little effort. A proper meal takes time, the conversation isn't rushed, and whoever is sat at the table is an equal among equals. Sharing food like this with new acquaintances is an incredible way of building relationships and countering the feelings of loneliness and isolation we can all experience.

Who are the lonely in your midst? Who has just moved on to your street? Who is new at work or doesn't fit in at the school gate? Who is it that seems to be at the fringe of your friendship group, your church community or clubs you attend? Invite them into your home, include them on your next friends' get-together, or maybe even invite yourself round for dinner if it is appropriate.

> Who are the lonely in your midst? Who has just moved on to your street? ... Invite them into your home

In all relationships there exists a power dynamic; who has the upper hand, who has control? Where does trust and mutuality fit in? When you are a host, you hold much of the power; you control the environment, the setting, how people feel when they enter the space, not just what they eat. You are largely responsible for the whole experience.

But Jesus was often the guest. When you are the guest, you are in a much more vulnerable position; you don't know what is expected of you. What is the etiquette or the norms for this place? Do you have to take off your shoes when you come through the front door? How will you know when you've outstayed your welcome? As a guest you do have one unique privilege, though – to affirm the efforts of your host. You have the power to put them at ease with their labours, to honour who they are and what they offer you.

At the heart of Christianity is the practice of sharing even the simplest of food with the expressed purpose of offering ourselves for the sake of others. Whether you are the host or the guest at the table, you can turn any meal into a redemptive and healing act of acceptance. You can witness to who God is and to the dignity of everyone gathered there. You can show everyone that all are welcomed to the table of the King of kings.

The table is set. Will you come? Who will you bring?

Competition breaks the ice

My sister, Chandni, and I enjoy cooking. We often search through food websites and old recipe books in order to concoct a tasty treat for the family. I started cooking five years ago and I have enjoyed every minute! I love the creativity of cooking and seeing the satisfaction on people's faces when they have eaten one of my delights. Preparing food means a lot to me because it is relaxing and peaceful.

My family enjoy inviting people around and sharing meals together. My parents want people to experience the love of Jesus in our home, and what better way to help them than around the table. On these occasions, Chandni and I enjoy competing against each other in cook-offs (shhh, just between you and me, I always win!) and apparently this playful rivalry helps break the ice for guests.

Carib Wings once generated some very 'healthy' competition. It is a simple recipe to tickle your taste buds with the right amount of heat, but also with classic flavours. I hope it will inspire you to open your doors to family and friends, and to get your kids involved in cooking too!

Enjoy!

Carib Wings Serves 3 to 4

Ingredients

1kg chicken wings

8 heaped tablespoons tomato ketchup

2 fresh green chillies

2 cloves garlic

4 tablespoons soy sauce

4 tablespoons balsamic vinegar

3 tablepoons Chinese 5-spice powder

2 teaspoons honey

4 sprigs thyme

Dash salt and pepper

A drop oil

1-2 teaspoons chilli flakes to garnish

4 spring onions to garnish

Method

1. Preheat oven to 200C/180C fan/gas mark 6.

2. Rinse chicken and place in a bowl.

3. Cut chillies and garlic and add them to your chicken.

4. Add tomato ketchup, soy sauce, balsamic vinegar, Chinese 5-spice, honey, thyme, oil, and salt and pepper.

5. Mix these ingredients until all the chicken is covered by the sauce.

6. Leave to marinate for 30 minutes.

7. Place in an oven-ready dish and bake in the preheated oven for 40 minutes or until the chicken is fully cooked.

8. Once ready, place in a serving dish and garnish with chilli flakes and spring onions.

A biblical breakfast feast

Kids love food – well, ours definitely do. They take after their parents, I guess! But let's be real, how often do we complain about this present age of endless technological distractions and lack of real face-to-face communication? At least when we watched TV as kids, with trays and dinner on our laps, we watched something together. But now everyone has their own personal device. As a family with a two-year-old and a six-year-old, our desire is to instil and demonstrate our value of family mealtimes.

We eat together several times a week and have created a list of family values in the kitchen. But more recently we have set aside a day where we have a home-made 'big family breakfast' involving the kids in the food choices and the cooking too. We have all the trimmings and treats and have music playing; it's a special occasion, including pancakes, bacon, waffles, fruits, maple syrup, French toast and yogurt, among other delights.

As we finish off our food, we go round the table thanking God for whatever comes to mind, but what makes our meals especially exciting is we then read a pre-planned Bible story or parable and discuss it. Our two-year-old maybe doesn't 'get' the conversation too much, but we involve her as we often act out the story, and she loves the songs too.

Discussions and songs around food are so relaxed and so much less intense. When the kids' cousins stay over, we will involve them too, which is a great witness of how we involve God in everyday life at our family feast of food and faith.

Healthy living is biblical living

Gluten-free, sugar-free, butter-free muffins ... I make this recipe once weekly for my husband and me. Healthy eating is important to me as my health-conscious father instilled this value in me as a young girl that our 'bodies are temples of the Holy Spirit' (1 Corinthians 6:19).

These muffins have also been able to bless others; for example, my friend just became a mother and I make them for her every week. She loves having a go-to healthy snack, being busy with a little one, and for me it helps me to take on the nature of a Proverbs 31 woman more and more!

'She is like the merchant ships, bringing her food from afar. She gets up while it is still night; she provides food for her family and portions for her female servants.'

(Proverbs 31:14-15)

Chocolate Muffins Serves 12

Ingredients

4 ripe bananas

⅓ cup coconut oil

¼ cup maple syrup or ⅓ cup coconut sugar

½ cup unsweetened apple sauce

1 egg

1 teaspoon baking powder

1 tablespoon baking soda

Pinch salt

1½ cups oat flour

½ cup almond flour

½ cup 70% dark chocolate chips

Method

1. Mash 4 ripe bananas.

2. Add ⅓ cup of coconut oil.

3. Add ¼ cup maple syrup or ⅓ cup coconut sugar.

4. Add ½ cup unsweetened apple sauce.

5. Add the beaten egg.

6. Beat together.

7. Add 1 teaspoon baking powder.

8. Add 1 tablespoon baking soda.

9. Add a pinch of salt.

10. Add 1½ cups of oat flour.

11. Add ½ cup of almond flour.

12. Mix together.

13. Add ½ cup of 70% dark chocolate chips.

14. Bake at 180C/160C fan/gas mark 4 for approx 25 minutes or till toothpick comes out dry.

'On this mountain the Lord Almighty will prepare a feast of rich food for all peoples, a banquet of aged wine – the best of meats and the finest of wines'

Isaiah 25:6

Go for it!

GAVIN CALVER

'it's not the quality of the cuisine that matters; it's about making the time and effort for the sake of others'

The church has a fantastic heritage of using food to help share the gospel – the recent global explosion of the Alpha course, with its key component of a shared meal, being just one of many great examples of this. That's why I'm delighted with the vision and passion behind *Simply Eat*. The collection of thoughts and recipes gathered together in this book provide something for everyone, and I hope these amazing stories will inspire us all with great new ideas for how to share the gospel. From a shared snack on the move to a full-blown three-course dinner party, we can all use food in a powerful way for Jesus.

In *Simply Eat*, we have seen that Jesus spent loads of time sharing life with people as He shared food with them. In doing this, Jesus showed that there's a clear connection between witnessing and hospitality. He also knew the value it places on another person when we sit down to eat with them, as shared meals provide more time for community and friendship-building than rushed interactions. This book wonderfully combines two of my primary passions – talking about Jesus and eating – and can help all of us in doing outreach like Jesus.

I've been involved in evangelistic ministry for more than twenty years, and some of the best moments of witnessing to others have happened over food. There's the time, many years ago, when an old friend surrendered his life to Jesus on a park bench, having just finished our doner kebabs at 2am after a night out. Or the moment when I was able to witness to some people who would never otherwise listen to anything about Jesus, simply because we were having a community barbecue. Time and time again I've seen firsthand what Jesus demonstrated in His ministry – sharing food opens doors of opportunity to share the good news!

My simple encouragement to you is to go for it. The type of food doesn't matter; what counts is making an effort to provide others with something to eat – and a potentially life-changing conversation! Don't worry if you're not a culinary genius. My cooking skills fall well short of average, but it's not the quality of the cuisine that matters; it's about making the time and effort for the sake of others. And whether you're providing the food or not, there are still plenty of ways we can share Jesus; whenever my wife and I eat out, we try to ask the waiter if they'd like prayer for anything. It's simple, but it could make all the difference.

People often ask me, 'How do you even start a conversation about Jesus?', and my first tip would simply be to ask questions of the other person. There's a cheesy but important saying: 'Popular people aren't interesting, they're interested.' Be interested in others, ask them questions, and soon enough they will ask one back. The most questions I've ever had to ask before being asked one back is seven, so, as long as it takes, do keep asking questions as it will give you the opportunity to share the life-changing hope you've found in Jesus! But don't forget that we're not asking questions and then simply waiting for the moment to speak ourselves; we must be engaged listeners, hearing the stories of others, and praying for Jesus to break in and transform lives.

Important though the food is, we know it's ultimately not the most essential ingredient – we want to be able to share our stories of what Jesus has done. The power of story is so underestimated, and the one you carry is as compelling as any other. While you sit and eat, share what a difference it makes to have Jesus in your life. What has He done in and through you that has transformed you?

So, as you put this book down today, I challenge you to choose who you want to invite, decide what you're going to cook, and then get praying for a fruitful time together! It might start with a hearty curry or a freshly baked loaf of bread, but the impact Jesus can have in the lives of others goes far beyond that! Know that He is with you, be brave, get praying, and go for it!

RECIPE INDEX

COPYRIGHT INFORMATION

Robert W Jenson, *Systematic Theology,* vol. 2, The Works of God (New York and Oxford: Oxford University Press, 1999), page 185

Wendell Berry, *What Are People For?: Essays,* 'The Pleasures of Eating' (Berkeley: Counterpoint, 1999), page 146

Walter Brueggeman, *Sabbath as Resistance* (Louisville, KY: Westminster John Knox Press, 2014), page 3

PARTNER ENDORSEMENTS

'At last a resource is in print that helps us grasp the fact that Jesus' life was a lot around eating with people. So much so that His critics accused Him of being a glutton and a boozer (Matthew 11:19). I really believe this book will help us walk a bit more as Jesus walked (1 John 2:6).'

Steve Bell, Director in Great Britain and Ireland, Interserve

Interserve exists to equip local churches to reach out cross-culturally with confidence and humility to bring lasting change in their communities

www.interserve.org.uk

'Simply Eat is a delightful and inspiring book full of stories of everyday Christians using hospitality and food to get to know their neighbours, to build friendships and to share Jesus. With mouth-watering recipes from around the world, this book will encourage you to reach out across cultures, and we pray that as you do, many will come to hear about Christ.'

Jo Sutton, Director of Communications, London City Mission

London City Mission has been sharing the good news of Jesus with London's least reached people for 180 years and supporting churches to open new doors for evangelism

www.lcm.org.uk

'Simply Eat is a wonderful book full of fabulous examples of how to build strong friendships with people of all faiths and none whilst sharing the hope and joy of knowing Jesus Christ. This high-quality resource will be a great encouragement for Christians unsure of how to get started and an inspiration to those seeking new ideas.'

Andrew Smith, Director of Interfaith Relations, The Church of England – Birmingham

The Church of England – Birmingham is made up of people from all walks of life who love God, follow Jesus and have made Birmingham their home

www.cofebirmingham.com

'We are committed to mission and inspiring others to mission. This new resource creatively encourages believers to share their faith with friends and family in a friendly non-threatening way.'

Steve Uppal, Senior Pastor, All Nations

All Nations is a thriving, ethnically diverse church in Wolverhampton that is passionate about mission in the UK and globally

www.allnations.org.uk

'Great Commission is all about equipping and inspiring a passion to make Jesus known. That's why we love the vision of Simply Eat, *bringing people together to share good food and good news stories of Jesus. We're so excited to see how God uses this book to inspire hospitality, generosity and a hunger to see others come to know Jesus.'*

Gavin Calver, Director of Mission, Great Commission, Evangelical Alliance

Great Commission inspires Christians to make Jesus known and empowers them to do so by creating original content and signposting other organisations' resources

www.greatcommission.co.uk

'A key value of Asian cultures is that no one should have to eat alone – but in the West they often do. Simply Eat *is part of the solution to this problem, celebrating the power and joy of eating together as we share both our food and our lives with one another. And in the UK's often polarised multicultural and multi-ethnic society, coming around the table to eat together will be essential to building community, welcoming outsiders and making safe spaces to share the good news of Jesus Christ.'*

Manoj Raithatha, National Coordinator, South Asian Forum, Evangelical Alliance

The South Asian Forum supports Asian church leaders and works together with the wider church to reach the Asian community with the gospel

www.eauk.org

SIMPLYEAT

EVERYDAY STORIES OF FRIENDSHIP, FOOD AND FAITH